Photography
A Practical Handbook

Allan Shriver

photography by Sylvester Jacobs

Galley Press

Designed and produced by
Albany Books
36 Park Street London W1Y 4DE

Copyright © Albany Books 1980

Published in the UK by
Galley Press
Euston Street Freemen's Common
Aylestone Road Leiceste LE2
7SS

House Editor: Lynne Pegden
Art Direction: Elizabeth Cooke
Design: Jaunita Grout

ISBN 0 86 136056 7

Printed and bound in Hong Kong

Acknowledgements

Thanks are due to the following
organizations for kindly allowing
their cameras and equipment to
be photographed for this book:

CZ Scientific Instruments
Lorell Photographics Ltd
Olympus Optical Co. (UK) Ltd
Pentax (UK) Ltd
Photomarkets (UK) Ltd
Photopia Ltd
Polaroid (UK) Ltd
J.J. Silber Ltd

A 35mm single lens reflex camera
with electronic flash unit.
(*Alan McFaden*)

Contents

Introduction

As Technical Editor of the magazine *Amateur Photographer* I have noticed a change taking place over the years in the way people view photography – a change which is only for the better. The mystique in which photography was once cloaked has been gradually slipping away. No longer is it an art too expensive and too rarefied for the amateur. There is a camera to suit everyone's needs and literally everyone can become a good photographer.

Unlike other hobbies, photography can be enjoyed any time of year, any time of day, any place. You can be alone or with friends. You can be large, small, agile or clumsy, young or old. There are no clubs that have to be joined; no prohibitively expensive equipment which has to be bought.

Most people are still reluctant to take their cameras with them wherever they go, yet with the modern, compact and efficient models available, a camera could always be at your side. People as a whole are taking better photographs. With more people using cameras than ever before, the quest for knowledge on all levels in photography is unceasing. Once you are familiar with your camera – and that is very important – you are ready to start shooting. Photography, perhaps contrary to what you have been told, *is* easy. Only a few simple facts need to be understood and the world is at your doorstep to be examined in endless minute detail before your lens. Yet, if you are confined in any way to remaining in the same spot, a whole world of photographic interest exists within your own home. You need not travel to the far corners of the earth to fully enjoy photography.

Those photographers with a little more knowledge can launch out and experiment with pictures until they need more advice from books, magazines or friends. Those who are

A 28 mm wideangle lens used close to this still life arrangement has produced an exaggerated perspective – objects at the edge tend to lean outwards; natural available daylight from a window prevents the subject from looking too much like a set-up studio shot and more spontaneous. (*Allan Shriver*)

just beginning to take pictures can always use a few tips on how to improve their photography easily – that is the purpose of these pages. If your failure rate increases, then simply go back over the main points again to refresh your memory, and take more pictures.

In short, to get better pictures, you must take pictures and study pictures. Study your mistakes. Study pictures in books and magazines. Read a photographic magazine regularly to pick up hints and tips from the pros and other amateurs. Join a photographic club or society if you are the gregarious type. Do not simply look at pictures – really study them. Ask yourself why you like them. Is there a 'clean' background? Is the main subject nice and big and bold? Are there no chopped-off heads or feet? Has distracting detail been cropped out? Has some special technique been used that you can easily master? Bear in mind that there are precious few special techniques that a professional uses that an amateur cannot.

If you remember only three words with regard to photography, your pictures should improve immediately – *identify, isolate* and *emphasize*. Next time, shoot your picture as you normally would, then take a second one, isolating and emphasizing the subject, and compare the results.

Just remember, you cannot become a good photographer by simply reading about it – you must practise, use up film, make mistakes and not be afraid to make them. Once you start to take photography too seriously, and even professionals do not do that, photography becomes a bore. When this happens – stop, or preferably, stop before it happens. Photography is simple and fun – fun above all. Even professionals sometimes just take snapshots.

This book is written more for the advancing picture-taker than someone who considers themselves a veteran photographer, so the first quarter of the book concentrates on explaining the few basic points which pave the way to better pictures. This is followed by a discussion of what to look out for when buying equipment and how best to select the right equipment for your needs. The second half of the book offers explicit tips to try out when shooting particular

subjects and types of pictures to help achieve success simply and without incurring a great deal of expense.

At first, do not be overly concerned with taking pictures which are technically or aesthetically perfect. Concentrate on improving both your technique and visual skills at the same time; try to avoid seeking one without the other.

Photography is for everyone – there is a

camera to suit everyone's ability and pocket (literally and figuratively). Photography as a hobby has no prejudice – everyone can make a mistake, everyone can take a good picture and everyone can have fun with it – and that is what it is all about.

A *Glossary* has been included at the end of the book. For your convenience, all entries

Good photographs can be taken on days of questionable weather as well as bright sunny days; low sun and atmospheric cloudy patches, whether due to rain, dust or fog, lend themselves to some superb moody landscapes.

in the glossary are italicised the first time they are mentioned in the text. Metric and imperial equivalents are given throughout except in cases where one is the standard accepted form of a particular photographic term.

Making a good picture

What is a picture for?

The communication power of photography is still underestimated and underused. Its potential is limited by our limited way of looking at it. Often it is viewed simply as a way to record where we went on our last holiday. While photography can cope very effectively with this, it is somewhat like driving a sports car at 55 mph (88 kmph) all the time. Unless we can understand and tap the potential of photography, we cannot possibly enjoy it, and ourselves, to the full. I hope that the following pages will open a few doors on a simple, yet highly enjoyable hobby in order that it may become more rewarding than simply a wistful flip through an album of holiday snaps on a cold winter evening.

Good pictures rarely happen; they are more often made – made by the thinking photographer. Many of us, including professional photographers, enjoy picture-taking with a simple and quick snapshot approach. However, if all our pictures are taken that way, few will be particularly good. Often it is just a small detail which makes the difference between a decent photograph and a really good one. A little knowledge of what can be accomplished and a few simple tips on how it can be done is generally all that is needed.

A good picture usually has one main message and this may be very obvious or quite subtle, depending on what the photographer wishes. As it has one main message, so too does it have one main purpose. A picture may be used to record: perhaps you need a picture of each wall in your home for insurance purposes to aid identification in the unfortunate event of a burglary. A picture may be used to remind: memories of last year's holiday wane alarmingly rapidly when one returns to work. A picture may be used to please: a photograph taken by you which you are proud of dresses up an otherwise drab wall. A picture may be used to amuse, entertain, provoke or inform. A good picture may even become, to some, an *objet d'art* in its own right. The good photographer will try to fulfil just one of these purposes with his or her photograph and not all in one go.

A good eye-catching and memorable picture has certain elements, as well, which should complement each other in order to suit the subject and intention of the photograph. Among these elements are an unusual viewpoint (especially if the subject is familiar); lighting to suit the 'mood' of the subject (harsh lighting for a dramatic effect and soft, diffused lighting for a romantic effect); a *composition* which leads the viewer's eyes across the picture and back again; a good exposure so that the light records the subject on film as you want it to appear on the photograph; a balance of approach to aid the validity or believability of the photograph (i.e. gentle flowing compositional lines, soft lighting and perhaps soft focus, too, for a flattering portrait of your favourite lady); and lastly, visual impact. Visual impact can be achieved by combining those elements listed above, but combined in such a way as to provide a meaning. This may be purely for the enjoyment of the photographer, or it may need to 'say something' to the viewer. Many photographers feel that if their pictures are remembered or have evoked thought, then they and the photographs have succeeded. They have set out to make a good photograph, not just click the shutter button when something 'nice' happened in front of their *lens*. Success often requires conscious determination.

Getting the right exposure

Getting the right exposure is half the battle; the other half is getting the picture sharply focused. These operations are both quite simple, yet are the main causes of discontent. Pictures are either too dark, too light or out of focus and blurred.

PAGES 12 & 13: Trees are used here as a frame for the picture and the stormy sky with shafts of sunlight breaking through gives a dramatic lighting effect.

RIGHT: If you planned to reconstruct the inside of an old Welsh woollen mill for a stage play set, a shot like this would serve as a record of the real thing. (*Anne Price*)

Most, but interestingly not all, successful pictures have a sharply focused main subject. Some simple cameras have a fixed-focus lens, so the photographer cannot change or choose the focus he requires anyway. Some cameras have automatic focus, so the photographer cannot do anything with these either. However, the majority of cameras have adjustable focus; with these the photographer must re-member to focus the lens on the subject each time he takes a picture unless the purpose of the photograph requires an out of focus subject. Some pictures are not pin-sharp because they have been taken through a *soft-focus filter* (a lens attachment), but the lens must still be focused as accurately as possible even for this effect. Some pictures of race cars or sportsmen may not be pin-sharp either, but this is usually

RIGHT: With a lighting quality near to that of an old Dutch Master painting, the light from the single window on the right was metered from the middle tones on the wall.

OPPOSITE: Since most of the tones here are of approxi-mately the same brightness and there are no extremes of highlight and shadow, the camera meter's suggested exposure can be relied upon. (*Anne Price*)

For indoor shots without flash, use the exposure setting combination of a wide lens aperture which should enable you to use a shutter speed fast enough to avoid subject blur through camera shake.

In high contrast lighting such as this, the best way to ensure correct exposure on the subject's face is to take a meter reading from very close or from the palm of your own hand.

intentional blur caused by subject and/or camera motion during the exposure, not by an out of focus lens setting.

Photographers sometimes say that when they 'take a picture' they 'make an exposure'. An exposure on film is necessary ultimately to make a picture – the film must be exposed to light *under controlled conditions*. Getting the right exposure on film is controlled by using two adjustments on the camera: the *shutter speed* and the *lens aperture*. If your camera is one of the more modern electronic and automatic types, one or both of these controls may be 'taken away' from you. In this case, your creative control is limited mainly to selecting and manipulating the subject, viewpoint and lighting.

Both the shutter speed and lens aperture control the amount of light reaching the film and therefore making the picture. Each also has a decided pictorial effect on the resulting photograph. If you use a fast shutter speed, you

will be able to stop or 'freeze' fast action such as a race car in motion. Accordingly, you can freeze slow action with a relatively slow shutter speed, whereas you must use a faster shutter speed to freeze faster action. The shutter speed controls the *time* during which the film receives image-forming light which is coming from the subject and passing through the lens.

A slow shutter speed for most purposes would be that of about 1/30 of one second which is expressed as 1/30 sec. This would not even be fast enough to freeze a person walking and is about the slowest speed which could be used while the camera is hand held without some extra steadying device such as leaning against a fence rail for support or using a tripod.

Cameras often have a range of shutter speeds, each of which is twice as fast as the speed before it and half as fast as the speed after it. For example, 1/250 sec is twice as fast as 1/125 sec but half as fast as 1/500 sec. Therefore the speed of 1/250 sec lets in half as much light to the film as

1/125 sec, but twice as much light as 1/500 sec. With careful manipulation of shutter speed you can 'stop' a race car or make a runner appear faster than a race car.

The lens aperture is similar to the human eye's iris; in fact, sometimes the lens' aperture mechanism is called an *iris diaphragm*. The wider the aperture, or opening, the more light passes through the lens to the film, and vice versa. On cameras with adjustable lens apertures, one aperture from a range may be chosen; these figures are also sometimes called *f/stops* or *f/numbers*. Each f/stop allows twice as much light through the iris as the f/stop before it, but half as much light through the iris as the f/stop after it. The bigger the f/number, the smaller the aperture size and so the less light goes through. For example, f/11 lets through twice as much light as f/16, but half as much light as f/8. The numbering scale is more or less arbitrary, so it pays to memorise the sequence for your camera.

The aperture not only controls the amount of light coming through the lens, but also the *depth of field*. This is the amount of detail in front of and behind the subject (on which you have focused the lens) which will also be in sharp focus. The smaller the numerical value of the f/stop (the wider the actual diameter of the lens aperture), the shorter the depth of field, i.e. less of the detail in front and behind the subject will look sharp. A large f/number (a small aperture) will allow much of the foreground and background to be rendered in sharp focus.

In picture taking, one control (aperture or shutter speed) must be sacrificed for the benefit of the other. Both must be balanced for the correct exposure, yet speed controls image blur while aperture controls the depth of field; usually the photographer must decide on whether he wants one or the other, or a compromise of a little of each.

A general rule of thumb for correct exposure is: in bright sunlight with the lens set at f/16, the correct shutter speed fraction is the reciprocal of the film's *A S A* number (marked on the film box) or that which is nearest to it.

With a strong horizontal and vertical line, neither has been placed exactly in the middle of the picture, to avoid the impression of two 'half pictures' in one.

Composition

Composition is one of the easiest ways to control what the photograph will look like in the end, yet is one of the more difficult things to get right. Although there is really no right way nor wrong way, some compositions seem better than others for a particular situation. What appeals to the photographer may not appeal to the viewer of his photograph, and vice versa. But with careful control, the photographer can make the viewer look longer at the picture and, as often happens, the more the viewer looks at the photograph, the more he likes it.

Composition is simply the arrangement of the various parts of the subject in the picture. These can be changed by moving the parts themselves or by moving the camera in order to give them a different relationship to each other. The latter method is the easier of the two, and often is the only practicable method. Avoid becoming a stiff-legged photographer; walk around the subject, kneel down or climb a wall to get the viewpoint you want.

Composition is related to the way we 'read' a visual image. Since we do not read a picture from left to right and from top to bottom as we would words on a page, it helps the viewer if you provide a comfortable visual route to follow so that he may see all that you intended him to see and re-read it more easily. Eyes prefer following smooth flowing lines or paths, consequently pictures which are easy on the eyes are those which have compositions formed like the letters C, L, N, O, S, U and Z and the triangular shape. So the main subject should lie somewhere along one of these 'vision route maps'.

The line of people has been used to develop a C-shaped composition around which the viewer's eye can travel while scanning the photograph from the balcony, down the wall, through the line and up to the balcony again via the flowering shrubbery.

OPPOSITE: The farm's winding lane is a good example of an s-shaped composition which serves as a route not only for the tractor, but also for the viewer's eyes.

20

Another photographic theory sometimes followed is called the *rule of thirds*. If the photo were divided by lines cutting the image into thirds vertically and horizontally, then the main subject should lie at one of the four points at which lines intersect. It has been proven that eyes of a portrait photograph are the details most often looked at and returned to by the viewer; so as the main 'subject' of a portrait photo the eyes should be 'placed' at one of the top two intersection points. Similarly the horizon of a landscape photo should never split the image in two more or less equal parts – it should be positioned about one-third from the bottom or one-third from the top. Just tilt the camera up or down a little more than usual. If you include the corner of a building in your picture which could divide the photo into two equal vertical halves, try to move yourself or the camera so that the edge is about one-third

in from either edge instead of right down the middle.

Composition also includes the choice of whether to take a photo in the horizontal or vertical *format* – unless your camera gives you a square *negative* or *slide*. Many of the 'old school' say that landscapes must be horizontal and action pictures must be taken in the vertical. While it is probably true that the horizontal format is more relaxing psychologically and the vertical format implies instability and therefore movement, the photographer may successfully choose either format if it suits the subject and the intentional presentation of the subject as either passive or active. A horizontal presentation might be fine for a calm, sunny, summer afternoon scene with cows grazing lazily in the pasture, but the vertical format might be more stirring for a stormy, dark, wintry landscape. However, there is no need to be overly con-

Colour impact

cerned by this because if you do your own printing or can get someone to do it for you, you can print only the section you want – say, the middle vertical third of a picture which you had originally taken horizontally.

Another compositional aid is the manipulation of the foreground. A good picture usually has depth as well as shape. Since a picture is a two-dimensional object, the impression of the third dimension, depth, can be imparted by the placement and treatment of foreground detail. With care, this can be part of the composition which helps lead the eye to the main subject. The most common technique is that of framing the main subject in an archway, in a gateway, in a window, or under the branches of a tree. So that the 'frame' does not demand too much attention from the eyes, it should preferably be slightly out of focus (by limiting the depth of field with a wide aperture), or slightly darker (by carefully selecting the lighting and viewpoint), or both.

ABOVE: The contrast in tone between the very dark and the very light areas is set off nicely by a splash of blue spread across the top.

LEFT: An otherwise dull shot of a row of grey houses is given added life by the inclusion of the spot of brilliant red colour struggling against the mass of greyness. (*Allan Shriver*)

Colour impact is one of the more subtle creative tools in photography. Just as shape, form, texture and pattern can be juxtaposed in a picture to make one stand out against the other, so, too, can colours be juxtaposed for impact. As most things are relative, we cannot judge the value of anything unless we have something else with which to compare it. With colours, a single bright colour looks bright only if it is surrounded by dull colours. Even if we have a picture which is predominantly made of hues of the same colour, i.e. baby blue, royal blue, navy blue, etc., no single hue would stand out, but if even a light shade of any other colour were included it would stick out like a sore thumb.

Pictures having hues of predominantly the same colour take on a sort of *monochrome* effect – like that of a black and white picture. We can use this 'trick of vision' to our benefit when composing a photograph. Take the example of a dark and stormy cliff-top seascape consisting of fairly muted colours. If you composed the picture so that even a small clump of bright yellow flowers appeared near one bottom corner, the whole picture would take on a fresh breath of life. A small spot of bright colour can be used to balance a larger expanse of dull tones of another colour. Similarly, a small spot of bright colour can counterbalance a larger area of a dull tone of the same colour, but not as effectively or dramatically as in the former example.

The success of the above examples depends on the *contrast* between different colours and/or the contrast between hues of the same colour; similarly, the angle of light falling on to the subject also controls the contrast of the colours. Light falling directly onto the front of the subject, as you are facing the subject, makes the whole scene look flat and dimensionless. However, when the light is moved to one side of the subject, shadows appear which not only add depth to the scene, but also provide visual contrast in the colours. You must have seen pictures taken in dull light compared to those taken in bright sunshine and noticed that the latter were more colourful. This is not simply because the latter had more light, since each picture would have received the correct exposure. Similarly, colours in landscapes always look less brilliant on hazy mornings than they do later in the day when the light brings out the colour brilliance better.

Colours can also add impact to a picture when they suit the mood of the picture. We often speak of a colour being warm or cool, e.g. warm yellow, cool green, etc. It is no accident that the description relates to temperature since each colour does have a temperature which can be measured in degrees *Kelvin* (K) precisely. However, the numerical temperature value is opposite to what you would expect, i.e. blue has a very high *colour temperature* (8000 K and higher), yet we speak of blue as being a cold colour. Orange has a low colour temperature (about 3000 K), yet we say that this is a warm colour.

Taking advantage of the psychological feeling or temperature of the various colours, we can emphasize the mood of the picture and the surroundings of the subject by placing hues of the appropriate colour in the picture. These may even be faked by placing coloured filters over the camera lens when taking the picture.

To have impact, a shot need not consist of a vast assortment of brilliantly lit colours; the impact here depends upon the softness in gradation between subtler hues of the same colour.

If your outdoors portraits always have very pale looking skin, then try to shoot these pictures when the sunlight is more 'warm' or yellowish/ orange, i.e. either in the morning or afternoon. If you want to shoot pictures at these times without the warmth of this light quality, place a light blue filter over the camera lens to balance the light back to 'normal'.

Due to the nature in which our eyes perceive colour, some colours tend to jump out of a picture while others recede. Red seems to jump forward; blue seems to recede; green lies somewhere in-between. We can use this to advantage when trying to add depth to a picture, e.g.

positioning red objects in the foreground.

Subjects in the distance of landscape pictures often look a hazy blue. This is due to atmospheric elements and a predominance of *UV* (ultra-violet) light between the camera and the subject. One way to cut through the haze and partially restore the natural colours of distant subjects is to fit either a haze, UV or Skylight filter on the lens. This also helps cut the bluish quality of colours photographed in the shade.

Black and white

Though most of us almost always use colour film these days, it is more challenging to succeed with black and white. This is because, without the colour to do much of the attention-grabbing work for us, we must manipulate other aspects of the photograph to bring and sustain life in our black and white pictures. The same elements should also exist in colour pictures, but we often let the colours themselves 'make' the picture. The subject elements requiring emphasis for successful black and white photos are texture, shape, form, tone and pattern. One works best when contrasted with another.

To put it simply, texture is either rough or smooth or somewhere between and, as before, is only rough when compared with something smoother. Some photographers enjoy shooting such stark subjects as peeling paint or a rough sawn plank or a row of glass bottles. Texture requires oblique lighting; frontal lighting

RIGHT: Showing texture;
35 mm camera; 50 mm lens;
50 ASA film; 1/125 sec; f/5.6.

OPPOSITE: Showing pattern;
35 mm SLR camera; 50 mm lens;
125 ASA film; 1/125 sec; f/11.

would render it flat, compressing the surface texture which only shows up when shadows exist between the high and low areas of the surface. Side lighting is best but try to make sure that there is enough light spread evenly over the entire surface you want to show.

Shape is the outline or silhouette of the subject. It is quite amazing how much feeling you can put into a photograph of people without showing any detail in the persons themselves, but simply representing them in silhouette. For the viewer, it is an easy type of picture in which he can mentally place himself – and association is a powerful tool of persuasion. Shape is best shown by light coming from the rear of the subject or *back-lighting*. Most automatic exposure cameras will give you a back-lit silhouette unless you adjust (increase) exposure to obtain some detail in the main subject. This is often used for taking portraits when trying to eliminate awkward backgrounds, but remember to give the picture the equivalent of about 1 or 1½ f/stops extra exposure by opening up the lens aperture or slowing down the shutter or a

little of each.

Form is captured best by carefully balanced lighting to enhance the subject's three-dimensional existence on a two-dimensional photo. But if only one light source is used (sun or flash for example) then try to position it 45 deg. up and 45 deg. to one side of the subject. Tone, too, needs careful lighting. Since we only have black and white, we must depend on a wide range of gradually changing tones of grey between them. A *slow speed* (low ASA number) *film* is best for this. The lighting need not be bright necessarily, but fairly even so that no great areas of dark shadow hide detail and form, though form does depend on some visible tonal detail in both shadow and highlight areas. Most important, there should be a very gradual shading through white, light grey, darker grey to black to best show form and tone.

Pattern can be quite easy to show, though pattern does not always mean repetitious pattern. It may be simply a recurring shape in various tones in certain parts of the photograph. For example, an s-shaped curve of beach huts

Showing low contrast; 35 mm camera; 50 mm lens; 400 ASA film; 1/1250 sec; f/4.

which follows the s-shaped curve of the edge of the seashore is a repeat of the seashore shape and as such is a pattern.

Black and white photos may benefit from the use of a *contrast filter*. The usual colours of contrast filters are blue, green, yellow, orange and red. When used on the camera's lens, each filter lightens the tone of subjects of the same colour and by comparison will darken the tones of the complementary colours, thereby increasing the pictorial contrast. For example, a red filter used on the lens would lighten the tone of a red car and darken the tone of a green field and a blue sky. So this is one way of controlling contrast in your black and white pictures. If you want a stormy picture on a calm day, then simply use a yellow, orange or red filter. The deeper the hue or darker the colour, the stronger the effect will be. A yellow filter will reveal light fluffy clouds against a medium 'grey' sky, while a red filter will show white and grey clouds against a practically black sky. The darker the filter, the more exposure must also be given to the photograph since the filter absorbs some of the light that passes through it. This is called the *filter factor* and is usually noted on the filter box. A filter factor of × 2 requires twice the usual exposure, therefore an increase of one f/stop (say from f/11 to f/8 at the same shutter speed, or from 1/250 sec to 1/125 sec at the same aperture).

Note: 1 A Skylight, UV or haze filter needs no exposure increase. 2 A camera with a TTL light meter or a light-reading cell on the front of the lens which would be covered by the filter when fitted generally needs no further adjustment since it automatically reacts to the light after it has passed through the filter; however, it may be 'fooled' by very dark filters. In this case, read the exposure necessary without the filter, make the filter factor adjustment and then fit the filter.

Special tricks

One of the most enjoyable aspects of photography is the vast range of visual effects which you can make with a minimum of effort and expense, and it is not necessary to master 'straight' photography before branching into the bizarre world of special effects either. You can start immediately, although it does help to know the basics of what makes a good picture (including exposure determination under tricky lighting conditions).

A quick look through any filter manufacturer's brochure will show the vast variety of special effect filters. You can use more than one if you like, but watch those exposures. The filters include the following:

pastels light hues for a slight overall colour cast

sepia slight brownish tint like that in old photos

single prism slightly stretches the image and gives rainbow-coloured fringes at the subject edges

BELOW: 35 mm SLR camera; 35 mm lens; 64 ASA film; 1/500 sec; f/5.6; with soft-spot lens filter fitted. (*A. Shriver.*)

ABOVE: 35 mm SLR camera; 50 mm lens; 64 ASA film; 1/250 sec; f/8; with star-burst lens filter fitted. (*A. Shriver.*)

multi-image prism, image-multiplier or *multi-facet prism* gives repeat images of your main subject

diffraction provides rainbow patches of coloured light around each bright light point source within the photo

starburst forms star-like rays of light around a bright light

cross-screen acts much like a starburst with bright lights, but can also provide a soft focus effect

sand-screen, soft-screen, soft-focus all soften focus for more flattering portraits

soft-spot softens focus at the edge of the picture leaving the centre detail sharp

fog provides a misty effect

polarizing eliminates reflections from shiny surfaces such as polished wood, water and glass, but not from metal, allowing you to photograph 'through' windows etc. without reflections

close-up enables you to get a larger picture of a small subject by getting the camera closer to the subject

split-field acts like half a close-up filter so half the picture is a small very near object filling half the camera's viewfinder frame while a larger distant object fills the other half of the picture

diffuser acts much like an overall soft-focus filter to 'hide' slight blemishes and 'hard' sharp detail – in skin and hair details especially – for a softer, more flattering portrait and 'dreamy' landscapes.

Cut-out masks or frames may also be held in front of the lens if you want a picture which looks as though it was taken through a hole, for example a keyhole or binocular effect.

For special colour effects, there are three main styles of graduated filters. All change hue or colour gradually from one edge of the filter to the other. For example, a graduated blue may change from blue to clear, or from dark blue to light blue, or from blue to red. A wide range of these types are on the market, so look around for just what you want.

You could also try a double exposure and so superimpose a friend's face in the sky over a field of flowers or perhaps put the same person in the picture twice. For this latter effect, first

cover the left half of the lens with a piece of black card and take a picture; then without moving the camera (using a tripod to steady it is best) cover the right half of the lens and take a second picture on the same frame of film (use the multiple exposure button or rewind button) but with the same person on the opposite side. You could also try 'sandwiching' two negatives together before you print them or have them printed by a processor, but let him know that this is the effect you want or he will think it is a mistake!

A night 'trick' you can try is to set your camera on a tripod and open the shutter for several seconds (with film of about 100 ASA) with the lens aperture at, say, f/11; anyone who walks in front of the camera will not show up provided they do not stop for very long in front of the lens. If you want a 'ghost-like' picture, set a small lens aperture so you also need a long shutter speed, say 6 seconds. Then ask someone to stand in front of the lens for about 4 seconds without moving and then to walk away from that position 'out of the picture'. You could also fake a night shot by shooting during the day, but under-exposing the scene with a very dark blue filter on the lens to simulate late night moonlight.

Should you want to fake a moving picture of a stationary subject and you have a *zoom lens*, place the camera on a tripod and use a fairly small aperture requiring a shutter speed of around 2 seconds. Then with the zoom focal length setting at one extreme end of the scale, operate the zoom ring towards the opposite end of the scale during the time the shutter is open. This will have an exploding effect on the main subject (which should be right at the centre of the picture). To simulate a soft focus or foggy effect without a special filter you could place a piece of fine net over the lens or breathe lightly on the front element of the lens.

35 mm SLR camera; 50 mm lens; 200 ASA film; 2 sec; f/4; with prism lens filter fitted. (*Allan Shriver*)

Common mistakes

Do not be afraid to fluff a few pictures now and then because it is through mistakes that we learn. However, you should try to find out *why* they did not come out the way you wanted or expected them to. It is not always easy to identify the fault sufficiently to know what caused it, so I have listed a few examples here under the headings Mistake, Cause and Remedy. I have also divided them into problem areas such as those due to lack of camera care, problems due to the flash, general camera operating technique and accidental faults.

Camera Care Problems

Mistake Picture looks dull even though taken in bright light.
Cause Front or rear surface of lens is dirty or dusty, which lowers image contrast.
Remedy Clean the lens carefully with proprietary lens cleaning solution, foam, tissue or silicon impregnated cloth; afterwards protect your lens with a lens cap when not in use and/or always keep a Skylight or UV filter on the lens.

Mistake Picture has irregular bright (often orange or white) streaks.
Cause Film has probably been accidentally exposed to non-image-forming light (i.e. not coming through the lens) possibly due to opening the camera back before the film was rewound (with 35 mm film) or the camera back does not close tightly enough against the camera body so light leaks in to the film.
Remedy Have your camera checked by a professional repairman.

Mistake Picture shows longitudinal streaks.
Cause Film has probably been scratched during handling or by dirt caught in the velvet light-trap of the *cassette* (35 mm film) or dirt and/or bits of film are caught on the shiny film guide rails.
Remedy Do not take the film from its package until you are ready to load it into the camera and have your camera checked and cleaned by a professional repairman once per year.

Where unexpected subject movement is a possibility, it is better to first set a shutter speed fast enough to prevent subject blur and sacrifice the depth of field advantage of a smaller aperture.

Flash Problems

Mistake Pictures too dark or too light.
Cause Wrong lens aperture has been selected; or flash unit has not been set properly; or subject is out of maximum flash distance range.
Remedy Check for correct film speed and aperture settings on both camera and flash unit; check the operating distance range of the flash chosen aperture.

Mistake Only a vertical portion of the picture is correctly exposed – the edges are too dark.
Cause On cameras with focal plane shutters (such as single lens reflex cameras) the correct *X-synchronization shutter speed* has not been selected.
Remedy Check the correct x-sync shutter speed in a camera handbook; this is usually 1/60 sec and sometimes marked by x on the shutter speed dial.

Mistake Picture has correct exposure on

only part of the frame, with dark background and edges.

Cause Flash has not reached all subject portions.

Remedy Eliminate background while composing picture or open up the aperture for correct background exposure; also check that the flash coverage angle (width) is suitable for the focal length of the lens in use (most flashguns cover the view of a moderate wide-angle lens, about 35 mm on 35 mm-film using cameras; also ensure flash lead is plugged into correct co-axial socket (marked x for electronic flashguns).

Mistake People have red eyes.

Cause Flash unit too close to camera lens and as people look towards the camera (in a dim room when pupils are dilated), light is reflected from the back of their eyeballs and reflects the colour red (of the blood at the back of the eye).

Remedy Move the flash away from the lens, up and to one side – even a few inches or centimetres helps; use a flash extension lead or a flash cube extender, ask subject to look away.

Mistake Subjects have overall colour cast similar to colour of interior walls or ceiling.

Cause Light from the flash bounced off the ceiling or wall on to the subject will be slightly tinted by the surface's colour.

Remedy Avoid bouncing flash off strongly coloured surfaces or compensate by fitting correction filter over flash reflector head or camera lens.

Mistake Although camera and flash settings are correct, subject still comes out too dark.

Cause If using *bounced flash* technique, auto-sensor 'eye' giving correct automatic exposures not pointing at subject.

Remedy Wherever you point the flash, check that auto-sensor eye remains pointed directly at subject.

General Problems

Mistake Heads or feet are cut-off; tree branches are sprouting from subject's ears or telephone poles from subject's head; background is too 'fussy' and confusing so that subject cannot be very easily identified.

Cause Careless framing.

Remedy Before shooting, look carefully around the viewfinder frame at various parts of subject for distracting detail not really part of main subject; stand close to main subject so it is big in the frame and obvious; if camera's viewfinder has a bright-line frame with picture corner marks, ensure that subject is within the frame or it will not be completely in the picture.

Mistake 'Stretched' close-up portraits.

Cause Exaggerated perspective due to using a *standard* or *wide-angle lens* too close to portrait subject.

Remedy Stand farther from subject and have only central portion of negative printed, or use a moderate telephoto lens (say, between 90 mm and 135 mm).

Mistake Pictures taken with camera pointed towards sun are under-exposed (too dark).

Cause Bright direct sunlight has 'fooled' the camera, since the camera usually takes a light reading averaged from the whole frame.

Remedy When shooting back-lit portraits or scenes, either take a meter reading from a small portion of the scene in which you want correct

Using a daylight-balanced colour film indoors leads to an overall orange colour cast unless corrected by the use of a blue lens filter.

exposure and then back up and take the picture with those camera settings, or, if your camera has a back-light compensation control, set it to give about $+1$/stop or $+1\frac{1}{2}$/stops more exposure (however, remember to reset it afterwards).

Mistake Although lens was correctly focused, picture still looks fuzzy.
Cause Shutter speed was probably too slow for camera to be hand-held without other supporting aid.
Remedy In very dim light, either use flash or steady camera with a tripod (and use a cable or remote release device), or steady yourself and camera against a solid surface (nearby wall, tree, bench, lamp-post, etc.) and gently squeeze shutter release button.

Mistake Picture has not come out at all or is partially obscured.
Cause Part of camera case or strap or your

While most double-exposures such as this are accidental mistakes (and are quite rare on most modern cameras) this one, in fact, could be regarded as an interesting study of a mother with her children thinking of her home.

finger has strayed in front of camera lens; or film has not gone through camera (if whole film is blank).
Remedy After loading film, check that it is being taken up in the camera by noticing that the rewind knob turns when you wind on (35 mm cameras); with *rangefinder* cameras it is difficult to see exactly what is happening in front of the lens since the subject scene image is not viewed through the lens, so take care to remove the lens cap and prevent camera case, strap and fingers from straying in front of the lens.

Mistake Buildings' edges appear to lean inwards.
Cause When the lens is tilted upwards to include tops of tall buildings, the exaggerated perspective creates 'converging verticals' effect.
Remedy Either forego including tops of tall buildings or stand close to the bottom of the building and shoot nearly straight upwards to exaggerate the effect; alternatively, if your camera takes interchangeable lenses, you can use a special lens (fairly expensive) called a

wide-angle shift lens.

Mistake Background detail is too sharp and too much foreground appears so main subject is lost.

Cause A very small aperture was used so depth of field was too great, bringing too much detail into sharp focus.

Remedy Shoot using a smaller f/number (wider aperture) next time, but take care to focus correctly on your chosen subject.

Mistake Picture shows one or more geometrical shapes of lighter tone of uneven and

Intruding bystanders must be tolerated at open events such as this so choose your moment of shooting carefully to avoid an obscured subject or a rather interesting cap bobble.

various colours.

Cause Flare is caused by light shining directly into camera's lens.

Remedy Stand so light does not shine directly into lens; fitting a *lens hood* also helps, but does not completely eliminate flare if you point camera directly at light source.

Picture-taking aids

Choosing a camera

Since there are about three hundred models of different types of cameras to choose from (not counting roll film medium format cameras), it pays to know a little about the camera types, their functions and capabilities before you set out to buy one.

Cameras are classified in terms of the picture or film size they take and whether or not the photographer can view the image of the subject as the lens sees it. The two main operations of a camera for successful pictures are the focusing and exposure settings. Correct focusing ensures a sharp picture, while correct exposure ensures that it is not too light nor too dark. Focusing is accomplished by one control – the lens' focusing ring. Exposure is controlled by adjusting both the lens aperture and the shutter speed.

The first decision you must make is which of these adjustments you would like to retain control over and which you would like the camera to set automatically for you. You can get wholly automatic cameras, wholly manually operated cameras and cameras which are automatic but with the facility to allow you to override the automatics and make your own settings.

Next you should decide what you plan to do with the pictures you intend to take. Are you going to get postcard-size prints made for passing around among friends or to paste down in an album or scrapbook? If you plan either of these, then you have a wide variety of cameras to choose from, but the most likely ones to appeal to you would be one of the *110 format cameras*. These yield a negative (or slide) which measures only 13 × 17mm, so its print quality is limited to medium/small blow-ups, though some of the more expensive models with high quality lenses can yield quite acceptable 8 × 10in (20.3 × 25.4cm) prints.

Most 110 models are very simple to operate, though the format boasts two quite sophisticated models, both single lens reflex (SLR) types. The cost of 110 models also varies considerably, so shop around until you find just what you want. Most have no controls or just one or two simple controls for exposure and/or focusing. These may be simple controls with subject symbols for focusing on close-up, middle distance and far distance subjects and/or sunny and cloudy cartoon symbols for exposure control (these may affect shutter speed, aperture or both to some extent).

110 film comes in a small plastic *cartridge* which is simple to drop in to the back of the camera and easily taken out again when the film is finished. This is one of its advantages, since some amateur photographers may find it difficult or annoying to have to load a cassette film (such as the 35mm types).

110 cameras may be sub-divided into five groups: the first is that with a single lens (many also being a non-adjustable or fixed focus type) with manual exposure control or limited automatic control. This group has about fifty models to choose from. They are among the simplest

Accessories may be the more expensive items such as extra lenses, flash, autowinder, bellows etc., or inexpensive items such as lens filters, cable releases, reversing rings etc.

A conventionally shaped 110 format camera with dual lenses and an integral electronic flash unit.

to use, but results may be a bit haphazard if you like to always take your camera with you and shoot indoors without flash and outdoors under bright sun.

The second sub-division has about twenty models to choose from, all of which have two lenses and manual or limited automatic exposure control. One of the lenses is a standard lens giving a view of the subject equivalent to normal human eyesight. The second lens, which tends to be selected by sliding a little bar switch across the front of the camera, is usually a telephoto lens, but in some models is a close-up lens. Watch carefully for the exact type you will need to use most often if you buy a dual-lens 110 camera.

More convenient for many photographers would be a camera from the approximately thirty-five-model sub-division of 110 cameras which have built-in *electronic flashguns*. These are small and not very powerful, but serve a useful purpose as an 'emergency' light source when you are caught out with not enough light for your picture. These flashguns are actually

built into the camera body, but many other 110 camera models also have matching detachable flashguns, so look out for the best one for your own requirements when choosing a 110 camera to use with flash.

Of course if you would like to have the best of both worlds, you could choose from the group of about twenty models of 110 cameras which have both a dual-lens facility and an integral flashgun. All these models so far have fixed exposure systems or limited manual control possible by the photographer.

Also check on all 110 format cameras if you can use both the more conventional 80 ASA/100 ASA films as well as the high speed 400 ASA films. This will be important if, for example, you do not want to buy a 110 with flash, but may still wish to use the camera in dim light situations such as for indoor portraits.

The last sub-division of 110 format cameras is those with built-in motordrive. This means that after every picture you take the camera will automatically wind-on the film to the next frame after you release your finger from the shutter button. At the moment, only about four models of this type are available in the 110 film format.

126 cameras use 126-size film which yields a

square negative measuring about 28×28 mm. However, due to the decreased size and weight of the 110 format camera models and their almost equally simple mode of operation and picture quality, their advantages have virtually killed 126 camera manufacture. A much wider choice of 110 format camera exists. All the 126 cameras have fixed focus lenses and fixed or limited adjustable control for exposure.

35mm cameras are the most popular and comprise the largest group for which the largest choice of film types also exists. The 35mm camera group has two main sub-divisions: *reflex* and *non-reflex cameras*. Reflex means that via a mirror and condensor/focusing screen aids, you can view the subject before you take the picture exactly as the camera's lens will see the subject when you press the shutter button to take the picture. The

35mm SLR (single lens reflex) camera is the most popular 35mm camera, since modern technology has made it both easier to use, more accurate and dependable. Many SLRs are the basis of a camera system and as such the photographer can later buy a wide selection of accessories to use with the SLR as his interests in special subjects grows. Close-up pictures, for example, benefit from the use of close-up aids and a wide variety of types exists to help the photographer who is interested in shooting small subjects magnified enough to completely fill the space of the film frame.

The 35 mm SLR group may be further divided into five main groups depending on their mode of exposure (almost all models have built-in exposure meters): Manual Exposure SLRs – the

A 35mm single lens reflex camera with electronic automatic exposure control.

A 35 mm rangefinder type camera with automatic and
manual exposure modes with a flashgun mounted.

photographer must read the light meter and
adjust lens aperture and shutter speed manually until the meter indicates that correct
exposure will result. Aperture-Priority Automatic Exposure SLRs -- the photographer must
set the lens aperture desired and the camera
will automatically select the shutter speed
necessary for a correct exposure, and most of
these models may also be used in the manual-
exposure mode if the photographer wishes;
Aperture-Priority Auto-Only SLRs – these
work in the same way as the former group of
cameras except that they cannot be used in the
manual mode (the photographer cannot select
a shutter speed of his choice other than by
adjusting the lens aperture to achieve that aim).
However, one model does have the facility to
be used with a plug-in accessory to make the
manual exposure model possible, so that the
photographer can choose his or her own shutter
speed and aperture; Shutter-Priority Automatic
Exposure SLRs – the photographer must select
manually the shutter speed of his or her choice
and the camera then selects the lens aperture
which will result in a correct exposure, all

these models have *manual exposure override* –
the photographer can choose to set both shutter
speed and lens aperture manually; Multi-
Mode Automatic Exposure SLRs – these models
offer the photographer the choice of automatic
exposures in either the aperture-priority or the
shutter-priority mode along with manual exposure override. Some serious photographers
prefer these cameras since a non-variable
shutter speed is required most often for action
and sports photography, while a non-variable
lens aperture is required for other types of
photography to control the depth of field.

35 mm non-reflex cameras are also called
35 mm *compact* cameras or rangefinder cameras
since focusing is not accomplished while looking at the subject image as it comes through the
lens, but as it is presented by a direct vision
viewfinder. The subject is focused by turning
the lens' focusing ring until the viewfinder's
two partial images coincide. Some compact
camera lenses simply have focusing symbols,
one to be selected on the lens according to the
subject's distance. These are usually a one
person head-and-shoulders symbol, a group of
people symbol and a mountain symbol.

Some models may also have sun, cloud and
sunny-cloud symbols for a modicum of manual
exposure control by the photographer. Exposure modes may be fully automatic or partly
automatic and may or may not have manual
exposure override for full photographer control
of the lens aperture and shutter speed settings.

35 mm non-reflex cameras have about five
main sub-divisions. Among the simplest types
to use are those with manual exposure or with
fixed exposure; the former group requires the
photographer to set lens aperture and shutter
speed, while the latter group has most of the
controls (focusing and exposure) already fixed
and of non-adjustable type. About fifteen
models are made in this group.

However, there are about forty models of
automatic exposure 35 mm compact cameras,
and about nine models also offer the handy
facility of manual exposure override. Most of
these need manual focusing, though simple
types may have focusing symbols in addition to
or instead of distance figures and/or a range-

finder focusing aid in the viewfinder.

Around twenty models of 35 mm compacts come with built-in electronic flash units. These are usually somewhat brighter than those built into some 110 format cameras, but are nevertheless not terribly powerful and should be relied upon only as an 'emergency' lighting source, though they work adequately for the usual type of indoors snapshot.

The latest technical innovation in camera design offers photographers the automatic focusing facility. About seven 35 mm compact cameras are of the autofocus type. All have integral flash units. These cameras focus their own lens (as well as providing correct exposure) automatically a split-second after the shutter button is depressed and before the shutter actually opens to take the picture.

Other features about the lens focusing vary considerably. Most focus the lens by a tri-angulated system of comparing the contrast of the light on the subject as seen by two windows at the front of the camera. One model uses an

An instant picture camera of the folding type with the automatic exposure and autofocus facilities.

A 35 mm compact camera with automatic exposures, automatic film advance and rewind and automatic focus.

infra-red light beam for the same purpose – this means that you can achieve correct automatic focusing even in a considerably darkened room (of course the integral flash provides enough light for correct exposure in the darkened room). One has true manual focus override whereby the photographer can set the lens

focus distance he or she requires. A few models also have an alternative feature of pre-focus memory; a button is pressed once to focus the lens and must be pressed again to actually take the picture. Only one of these models allows the photographer to cancel the pre-focus memory if he changes his mind. The infra-red autofocus model has the additional feature of a built-in automatic film advance winder and rewind motor, too.

Instant-picture cameras have the advantage of yielding a fully developed photo in a few minutes. They are relatively lightweight, though bulky to carry. Film packs are limited to a maximum of 10 shots, work out more expensive than conventional film in the long run and must be specially copied for a repeat image since no negative exists from which to make another print. Types of film have advanced considerably from the peel-apart variety of some years ago, which needed a messy coating from a smelly applicator, to the modern convenient dry-process one. Today's models have prints which come out of the camera immediately after the picture is taken and need no further attention – you can watch the image develop before your very eyes, which is part of the magic of using an instant-picture camera. Exposure control is still often problematic in most but the very expensive models, though some of the more sophisticated types offer a built-in electronic flash while two models have the autofocus feature (which is yet another system based on the use of an ultrasonic sound wave).

Choosing a film

You can always get a black and white picture from a colour film, but not vice versa, which is one good reason to shoot in colour. As the cost of colour negative film processing and printing increases, it also makes more sense to shoot colour slides (*transparencies*). However, if you shoot slides, you will need a projector and a projection screen to look at them – unless you are content with passing around a hand slide viewer which magnifies them only slightly. If you purchase a daylight projector you can view them without a projection screen as it will have a built-in screen of about 10 in (25.4 cm) square.

When buying film, it is important to specify the *film speed* or ASA number. This is the film's sensitivity to light: the higher the ASA number, the more sensitive it is, so the easier it is to take pictures in dim light. A 25 ASA film is a 'slow' film and needs lots of light, while a 400 ASA film is 'fast' and needs less exposure – in fact, 16 times less light than a 25 ASA film. For example, in a home's normal lounge lighting, a 25 ASA film would need an exposure (without flash) of about f/2.8 at 1/2 sec (much too slow a shutter speed to hand hold), while a 400 ASA film in the

Film varies as to whether it gives black and white or colour pictures, negative or positive images, and by its sensitivity to light (ASA rating).

A fast (or high ASA number) film was up-rated for greater dim light sensitivity which also shows increased grain. (*Allan Shriver*)

same circumstance would need an exposure of about f/2.8 at 1/30 sec (just fast enough to avoid subject blur through camera-shake with a hand-held exposure).

The ASA speed also affects the size of the *grain*. Grain refers to the little particles of silver in the film which record the subject's image when affected by light and processing chemicals. A slow speed film is also said to be a fine-grain film, while a fast film yields pictures with larger more noticeable grain.

Colour negative films may be exposed quite successfully to light of almost any colour temperature (sunlight, electronic flash, indoor *tungsten* and fluorescent lighting); however, *colour slide* film is 'balanced' or adjusted for correct colour reproduction only when exposed to daylight *or* tungsten lighting, so one of these two types should be specified when you buy slide film. If daylight-balanced film is exposed to tungsten light, yellow pictures will result; if exposed to fluorescent light, green pictures will result. Electronic flash has nearly the same quality (colour temperature) as daylight, but flash bulbs must be coloured blue. A colour correction/conversion filter may be fitted to the lens when film is exposed to light for which the film is not balanced to obtain faithful colour reproduction.

Choosing a lens

If your camera has the interchangeable lens facility, you can take a wider variety of pictures and with more special effects than with a standard or *normal lens*. However, some 110 format cameras may have a switch for selecting a built-in *telephoto* lens.

Every lens has three main functions: to focus the picture, to control the light passing through it, and to magnify or reduce the size of the subject. All interchangeable lenses have manually adjustable focus; however, although most lenses also have an iris to control the f/stop, each may have a different maximum aperture size. The smaller the f/number, the wider the aperture, the more light passes through and the easier it is to take pictures in dim light. The aperture size also controls depth of field as mentioned in earlier pages.

Subject magnification is effected by the *focal length* of the lens. Each format (110, 35mm, etc.) has its own 'standard' lens focal length – that which yields a view closest to that of normal human vision. The standard lens for the 35mm format is usually 50mm though is sometimes 55mm or 45mm.

A lens with a smaller focal length number, i.e. 28mm, has a wider angle of view so is called a wide-angle lens. With this lens you would not have to back away so far from a group of people to get them all in the picture, consequently it is ideal for family portraits in a small room. A wide-angle is sometimes also called a short focal length lens.

A lens with a larger focal length number, i.e. 135mm, has a narrower angle of view, so to fill the film frame with a smaller view it must magnify the subject. With this lens you can get a full facial portrait of someone standing quite a distance away. It is called a telephoto or tele or long lens, and the larger the focal length number, the more difficult it is to hold steady. A general rule of thumb is that the slowest shutter speed which is usable without getting camera-shake is the reciprocal of the lens' focal length (or the nearest speed); therefore the slowest possible hand-held speed for a 135mm telephoto lens is 1/135 sec, but the nearest speed setting is 1/125 sec.

A zoom lens has an adjustable focal length; for example, a 75–200mm zoom can be set at any focal length between those figures – 77mm, 93mm, 167mm, etc., the advantage being that you can choose the exact subject magnification desired. As negatives can be enlarged at the printing stage, this is a bigger advantage for photographers shooting slides which cannot be enlarged later except by a special copying process. You can also have fun by operating the zoom ring during a long exposure for an exploding-subject effect.

Four interchangeable lenses for a 35mm SLR (left to right): a zoom lens, telephoto lens, wide-angle lens and standard lens.

Choosing an accessory

Accessories can make it easier and quicker to take certain types of pictures. Some affect the appearance of the photo while others merely help the photographer operate the camera. If you are after an unusual shot, then one of the special effect filters mentioned earlier will do the trick. If you are unsure of the result, take a 'straight' shot first and follow it with the special effect shot.

A viewfinder rubber eyecup will help you focus better especially if you wear spectacles; it prevents stray light from the rear from lowering the relative brightness and contrast of the focusing screen's image. Most camera makers offer a range (usually −4D to +2D) of eyepiece correction lenses if you do not want to wear your spectacles. A collapsible rubber or plastic lens hood will help to reduce the chances of dull-looking *low contrast* photos by lessening the likelihood of flare ruining your pictures.

To take close-ups the simplest way is to use a close-up filter (supplementary lens) which simply screws on to the front of your lens. Usually available in four strengths of +1, +2, +3 and +4 dioptres, the higher the number, the closer you can get for greater subject magnification. A less expensive but slightly more complex way to get closer is with a reversing ring which allows you to mount your lens back-to-front on the camera. Or another type of ring allows you to mount a standard or wide-angle lens backwards to the front of your normally mounted standard lens.

Extension tubes fit between the lens and camera body for close-ups. They usually come in sets of three, each of increasing thickness. They may be used singly or together; the greater the separation between lens and camera, the greater the magnification. A bellows focusing unit acts like extension tubes, but it extends

Using a 75-260mm zoom lens at its maximum 260mm setting has 'squeezed' the planes of the subject together; even a long lens hood has not prevented blue spots of flare appearing on the against-the-light picture; this is sometimes seen in the viewfinder but not always to the extent with which it will appear in the end photograph. (*Allan Shriver*)

farther for greater magnification and offers infinitely variable adjustment for just the right degree of magnification.

For sports pictures, a *teleconverter* is an inexpensive way to obtain a 100mm or 150mm lens effect from your 50mm standard lens by fitting a ×2 or ×3 teleconverter between the 50mm lens and camera body. An autowinder for continuous shooting at about two frames per second may also help your sports shots.

Night pictures are best taken with the aid of a tripod, monopod or table-top tripod (easier to carry) when used with a cable release. The heavier the camera, the heavier the tripod should be to keep the camera from shaking during the time exposures. The cable release is useful in that it allows you to fire the shutter without touching the camera, thereby avoiding the risk of blurring the subject.

Choosing a flash

Electronic flashguns have all but taken over from the little flashcube for most cameras, even instant-picture cameras. They give more light, last longer and are cheaper to operate in the long run, plus they are always there when you need them – you won't have to remember to buy more flashes.

The measure of a flashgun's strength is its *Guide Number* (GN). The GN is always related to feet or metres and a specific ASA number; a quite common small gun would have a GN of about 25 (metres, 100 ASA). A gun may be entirely manual, meaning you must set the camera's lens aperture to suit the subject distance for each shot, or it may be automatic which means you can set one aperture and as long as your subject stays within a given range, your pictures will be correctly exposed. Or the gun may offer both modes of operation or more than one aperture choice for auto operation. The most economical auto guns have what is called a *thyristor* which helps to save battery power as most guns are powered by AA-size batteries.

A common size of electronic flashgun which is fitted to an SLR camera's hotshoe and needs no x-sync lead connection.

Most small guns can be fitted to the camera's *hot shoe*, however if your camera does not have one, you can get an accessory shoe for the flash; then the flash must also be connected to the camera's flash synchronization socket marked x. If your camera has a focal plane shutter (such as that in an SLR), be sure to set the correct x-sync shutter speed; this will be noted in the camera handbook, but is usually 1/60 sec.

If you have a manual gun, then the formula by which you determine the required lens aperture setting is the following: the GN (in feet or metres) divided by the flash-to-subject distance equals the correct f/number (or choose the next closest f/number on your lens). Most guns have calculator dials to help determine the correct f/stop, but if you use this formula, then the GN and your flash-to-subject measurement units must be the same, e.g. both in feet. Some electronic shutter SLRs have *dedicated flashguns* which, when ready to fire, will automatically set the correct shutter speed and/or aperture for you.

Later, as your flash pictures get more sophisticated, you may like to get a flashgun having a bounce head or bounce reflector. Bouncing the light off the ceiling or a wall towards the subject gives a more natural effect and avoids the 'red-eye' problem. Whatever type of flashgun you have, the chances of red-eye can be reduced by using a flash bracket; this holds the flash connected to the camera, but some distance away from the lens. For this your camera must have an x-sync socket for the electrical connection.

Choosing a light meter

Although most cameras these days have a built-in light meter, there are times when a separate hand-held meter is helpful – most notably at night or in dim light indoors when you are not shooting with flash. These light meters have calculator dials which offer an at-a-glance range of alternative exposures (aperture and shutter speed combinations). From these you can select the combination which will yield a great depth of field so the utmost detail is sharp, or the one which will 'freeze' a fast moving subject.

The two main types of meters are the selenium cell meter which needs no battery and the Cadmium Sulphide (or CdS) cell meter which depends on battery power. The selenium cell meter is just as accurate as the CdS meter in average lighting conditions, but falters in dim light since it depends on light to activate its needle on the indicating scale of exposure figures. However, the CdS meter tends to 'remember' some of the previous readings if this was a bright light source. So if you take a CdS cell meter reading in dim light directly following a bright light reading, allow a half a minute to elapse. This also holds true for SLR cameras with CdS cell meters.

Meter readings may be taken by the *reflected* or *incident light* method. The former measures the light which is reflected by the subject and the latter measures the light falling on the subject. Cameras with built-in meters measure reflected light. Reflected light readings are taken from the camera position with the meter pointing to the subject. Incident readings are taken from the subject position with the meter pointing to the light source. Only special flash meters react fast enough to measure the output of an electronic flash, (usually at 1/1000 sec), but these meters are quite expensive.

An incident light reading is technically more accurate as it measures the scene illumination so that the subject is recorded more naturally, without the meter being influenced by very dark or very light subjects. Such accuracy is of value particularly when shooting colour slide film. Not all light meters can take incident light readings, so check this – if one does, then it should come with a diffuser bubble or cone.

A camera's meter takes an average reading from the whole scene. If it is unduly influenced by, say, a blindingly bright beach, you could get a dull looking day in the resulting picture; similarly, if you take a back-lit portrait shot, the result will be a silhouette, unless you compensate by giving extra exposure (about $+1\frac{1}{2}$/ stops). If, on the other hand, you shoot a spot-lit actor on a dark stage, he is likely to appear totally white with the stage as a grey background. The solution is to give the shot about -1/stop less exposure than the meter indicates.

Processing a black and white film

If you have a small room or closet which can be made light-tight for about two minutes, then you can easily develop your own film; black and white film is the easiest and quickest of all. Once developed, what you have is negative film which then needs to be printed on to paper for a print; however if you process your own slide film all you need do then is to separate the images and put them into mounts. Processing your own film makes your photography more economical and much more fun.

Only two chemicals are needed to develop a black and white negative film. You may find their smell a bit obnoxious at first but both are quite harmless. However, you should keep them well out of the way of children. These two chemicals are called *developer* and *fixer* (if you reuse your fixer, a *stop-bath* solution will help extend the fixer's life, but this is not absolutely necessary).

Very little special equipment is needed.

This sophisticated CdS cell hand-held exposure meter can be used for both reflected light and incident light readings.

ABOVE: Careful control of film development time and temperature as well as the choice of chemical helps control the end result.

OPPOSITE: Only a few small and fairly inexpensive items are necessary for developing your own black and white films.

The minimum requirements are a film developing tank, a film loading spiral and a thermometer. Some spirals are adjustable so that they take several sizes of film (though not at the same time). Some tanks will also take more than one film at once which saves time if you have several films.

The whole process depends on controlling time and temperature – the time the film is in each solution and the temperature of each solution. With black and white film the solution temperature is generally 20 deg.C (68 deg.F). However, it is not critically important if you are 2 to 4 degrees above or below this although the best results are had from explicitly following the times and temperatures noted for your film packed with the developer.

A common processing time from preparing the solutions to the dry film may be as long as one hour, but this includes a washing and drying time which does not require your strict and constant attention. The total time the

film may be in the chemicals is usually about 10 minutes, though this varies with the film and developer type.

The main steps you need to remember are developing; fixing; washing; drying. However, you could insert a very short plain water rinse or stop-bath rinse between the developing and fixing steps, but this is optional. The film must be removed from its cartridge or cassette *in total darkness* or the whole film will be ruined, but once the film is loaded on to the spiral and the spiral is in the tank with the lid securely on the tank, the rest of the process can be done in normal room lighting. The chemicals for black and white processing will not hurt your sink's drain, but give it a good flush with clean water afterwards if for no other reason than to get rid of the smell.

Tackling different subjects

Outdoor pictures

Outdoor pictures are probably the easiest to take in that we can follow the old adage 'stand with your back to the sun' and click away. The only trouble with that is that your subject, if it is a person, will be looking directly at the sun and therefore squinting like mad. What you should do is stand them and yourself at an angle of 45–90 deg. to the sun. If the sun is very bright, you can use a *fill-in flash* – this just adds a little bit of electronic flash illumination to lighten the darkest shadows. To prevent the flash from overpowering the sun and to avoid odd looking shadows, set an ASA number on your flashgun which is about four times higher than the film number, for example with 100 ASA film in the camera, set the flashgun calculator dial to 400 ASA. (And remember to use the correct x-sync shutter speed, too!)

One alternative would be to shoot with your subject's back against the sun; to get the correct exposure, you would then need to use your camera's *back-light compensation control* or give the picture an extra $1\frac{1}{2}$/stops of exposure from the metered reading, by opening the lens aperture, say, from f/11 to between f/5.6–f/8, or by slowing the shutter speed from, say, 1/250 sec to 1/125 sec *and* opening the lens by $\frac{1}{2}$/stop from f/11 to between f/11–f/8.

Another way to shoot people outdoors on a bright day without their squinting is to position them in the shade. To avoid a slight overall blue cast (due to the UV rays in the shady light) use a Skylight or UV filter on the camera lens.

Landscapes are made more dramatic when they have more visual depth. This can be accomplished by including some object in the foreground – but not so big, bright or sharply focused that it conflicts with the background for the eye's attention. The shady branches of a tree serve as a convenient frame for a distant scene. An archway, doorway, gateway or fence, would also serve the purpose. Also try to avoid getting the landscape's horizon dead-centre across your picture and the main subject in the landscape (a distant steeple perhaps) right in the middle.

Landscapes, too, can look dull and flat when taken with your back to the sun or by noon sunlight when light rays are coming virtually straight down and there are no shadows to give an impression of depth – the third dimension. So shoot when the sun is at about 45–90 deg. to your side. If you shoot early in the morning or later in the afternoon, your landscapes will take on a warm glow, since the colour temperature of the sunlight is lower at these times of the day. Early morning or late afternoon portraits exhibit a slightly warmer (tan) skin colour, too.

Try to use what you know of compositional shapes and lines to lead the viewer's eyes to your main subject. A classic example of this is a landscape which has an archway of trees at the top with the tree trunks at the left and right edge. At the bottom is a fence with a gate towards one edge. From the gate a winding (s-shaped) path leads the eye (upwards) into the distance where a country church steeple sits bathed in the glow from a shaft of sunlight peeping around the edge of a storm cloud.

The main element of a landscape does not always have to be in the background either, though is only rarely in the foreground. Avoid a background with so much detail that it distracts attention from your main subject. The reason I say your 'main' subject, is that you will have decided to take a particular picture due to a particular detail. But although this item will want to be fairly large in the picture, you should include some other detail to 'set the scene' or location of that item.

To avoid distracting detail, it is easiest to experiment with various camera viewpoints. Do not hesitate to climb up on a wall or fence or kneel down for just the right perspective on your subject. If you kneel down, then the sky will act as a good background (but watch that exposure). If you straddle a fence, the background will be the green grass instead of a

PAGES 50 & 51: Rangefinder type 35mm camera; 50mm lens; 160 ASA film; 1/60 sec; f/8.

OPPOSITE: Rangefinder 35mm camera; 50mm lens; 200 ASA film; 1/25 sec; f/8 *(Anne Price)*

ABOVE: Composition is an important factor in taking good pictures. 35 mm SLR camera; 180 mm lens; 160 ASA film; 1/250 sec; f/11.

OPPOSITE: Picture taken indoors, making the most of available light. 35 mm SLR camera; 50 mm lens; 160 ASA film; 1/60 sec; f/4.

wild mixture of buildings, people, cars, telephone poles, trees and fences – all items which would compete with your main subject for attention.

Another way to make your subject stand out from a crowded environment is to shoot using a fairly wide lens aperture, say f/4. This limits the depth of field, so although foreground and background detail is included, it will be so out of focus as to be unrecognizable. To do this, first set the fastest shutter speed you can, then while you watch the exposure meter indication in the viewfinder, turn the lens aperture until you get a correct exposure signal.

Available light pictures indoors

Indoor pictures always look more natural if you can take them by the *available light* and not use flash – try to use flash only as a last resort. The classic Dutch painters devoted lifetimes studying and recreating scenes on canvas by available light, but after seeing your results from a few rolls of practice film you will be well on the way to judging not only what exposure is required but also the contrast range of the

Rangefinder 35 mm camera; 50 mm lens; 200 ASA film;
1/15 sec; f/2.

light on your subject.

One of the more difficult abilities to develop in photography is to see the changes in lighting brightness and contrast range on your subject. This may be easier to do by looking through the camera's viewfinder since the scene will appear more two-dimensional and picture-like there.

To judge what exposure to use, take several light readings if you do not have to act quickly to catch a fleeting subject. First meter the darkest area in which you want to see some detail, then meter the lightest area in which you want to see some detail. You may then choose to use the exposure setting between these two readings. If the first reading recommended 1/30 sec at f/1.8 and the second reading 1/30 sec at f/5.6, the mid-way exposure setting to use would be 1/30 sec at f/2.8.

Another method which you may feel suits your shooting style better is to meter the single

most important area where you want the most detail and use this exposure setting. Alternatively, you could compromise by selecting a setting between that given in the first example above (1/30 sec at f/2.8) and that in the example where you have taken just one reading.

Ideally the best approach is to ensure that the light on your subject is fairly evenly distributed and of about the same brightness. This is quite easy to do with a few simple aids. The darker areas of your subject can often be lightened by using a light toned object such as a white piece of cardboard, slide projection screen or a white sheet as a reflector. Position your subject at about 90 deg. to the light, then position your reflector on the dark side of your subject so it throws light onto that side. A helper is useful here, but a bit of card can be propped up on a chair or table top with books if need be. This is a good technique especially for softly lit indoor portraits relying on strong daylight coming through a window when your subject is positioned fairly near the window.

Since the light level is not usually so high or

bright as outdoors, you may find that you will need to use a fast film with an ASA rating of about 400 ASA, though 200 ASA would probably do also. Experiment: try one of each, find the one you like better and stick with it for results you expect to be consistent with your experience of judging exposure. With a 400 ASA film, you can probably shoot at f/2.8 at 1/30 sec in normal evening living room lighting. A faster shutter speed and/or a smaller aperture could be used during the day when sunlight streams in through the windows, especially if you can position your subject nearer the windows.

Remember, too, that you should consider not only the quantity of light but also the quality. If you are shooting black and white film, this is not a problem. However, if you are going to shoot colour film you must consider colour temperature. If you shoot by sunlight during the day indoors, then obviously a Daylight-balanced colour film is the correct one to use. If you shoot colour slide film, a fairly dark orange colour cast will exist on your slides taken by the normal room tungsten artificial lighting unless you fit a *colour correction* (CC) *filter* to your lens – a strong blue such as an 80 A. If you are shooting on colour negative film, complete colour balance correction is not absolutely necessary, though still desirable for the best colour reproduction. However, since a colour negative must be printed by an enlarger, some colour correction can be made at this stage.

Another alternative is to use a colour slide film specially balanced to produce faithful colours by light of a low colour temperature. Type B Tungsten-balanced film will be helpful when shooting by normal room tungsten light bulb lighting, though a slight yellow cast might still be present. A Type A Tungsten-balanced slide film is used when shooting by the light of photoflood lamps.

Another alternative to consider is artificially increasing the ASA rating of the film you are using. If you *up-rate* a 400 ASA film by one/stop it then acts like an 800 ASA film. Then you can use the next faster shutter speed or the next smaller lens aperture. In fact what you are doing is *under-exposing* the film by the equivalent of one/stop and compensating for this by over-developing – giving the film extra time in the developer. If you use a commercial processor, be sure to tell him the ASA speed at which you rated the film. Not all processors offer this special developing service. The up-rating technique can, however, be used on all films. The more you up-rate, the greater contrast you will have and the grainier the results will become.

35 mm SLR camera; 24 mm lens; 64 ASA film; 1/60 sec; f/5.6; direct off-camera flash. (*Robert Estall*)

Flash pictures indoors

If you must use flash to take your pictures indoors, they will look much more natural if you can use the bounce flash technique. This involves aiming the flashgun towards the ceiling or a wall and allowing the flash to be spread out more evenly by that surface. The result is that it cuts down on the very hard dark shadows often seen in pictures taken with the flashgun mounted directly on the camera. However, with some cameras this cannot be avoided.

Some flashguns can be left mounted directly on the camera's hot shoe while part of the flashgun's reflector is aimed upwards at the ceiling. In these cases, if the auto-eye sensor of the flashgun remains pointed directly at the subject, the gun can still be used in the automatic mode. Some guns do not have tilting

35 mm SLR camera; 100 mm lens; 25 ASA film; 1/60 sec; f/11; bounced flash. (*Adrian Knowles*)

reflectors but do have x-sync leads which allow them to be removed from the camera (connected only by the lead) and held in such a way that the reflector points at the ceiling while the picture is being taken.

For manual flashguns, the lens aperture will have to be calculated. To do this, simply divide the flashgun's Guide Number by the flash-to-subject distance. However, since the light has farther to travel than normally (first to the ceiling, then to the subject, then back to the camera), and since the ceiling or other reflecting surface will absorb some of the light, the lens aperture should be opened up about an extra + 2 f/stops wider then the original calculation. You could open the lens by + 3 f/stops if the ceiling is particularly high or of a dark tone. Also, be wary of deeply coloured reflecting surfaces as they will tint the light with their colour, which could be unfortunate if you are shooting portraits by this method. Try for a white, cream or beige coloured reflector for portraits specifically. Perhaps a friend could momentarily hold up a white card reflector near your subject to help you.

Another snag when shooting with flash indoors is to watch out for highly reflective surfaces such as glass objects, china, windows, mirrors, etc, which could throw an ugly reflection back into the camera's lens and perhaps spoil the picture. This happens most often when the flash is used directly on the camera.

Be careful, too, when you are using a wide-angle lens indoors. Not all electronic flashguns are designed to cover the area seen by all wide-angle lenses, although most will cover the angle viewed by a 35 mm lens (on the 35 mm film format) and others will cover the 28 mm lens view. Some flashguns are sold complete with a wide-angle diffuser attachment which clips over the reflector to spread the light out into a wider pattern. Some also have telephoto attachments to concentrate the light when shooting farther away from the subject with a telephoto lens.

Automatic exposure flashguns must be used with care, too. Because they are designed to shut themselves off when they give even light for an average toned subject, walls which are

very light or dark will 'fool' them. If the walls are specially dark, then it would be a good idea to set a film speed number on its dial of about twice the numerical value of the film speed you have in the camera. For particular light walls, set an ASA speed on the gun which is about half the numerical value of the film you are using.

Red-eye is probably the most common problem when shooting flash pictures indoors. It is easily cured, however, by not using the flash directly on the camera. Even if you can only hold it at arm's length up and to one side away from the lens (but pointing at your subject of course) this should be enough to eliminate red-eye. If for any reason you cannot do this, you will have to select shots in which your subject is not looking directly at the flash and camera lens. Sometimes the phenomenon does not occur so readily when the ambient light level in the room is fairly bright so that the subject's eyes are less dilated.

With just a bit more expense you can get really professional looking pictures indoors – you need two extra little flashguns (they do not need to be very powerful) and two *slave units*. A slave unit is a light sensor switch which

35 mm SLR camera; 50 mm lens with +2 dioptre close-up lens; 64 ASA film; 1/60 sec; f/11; direct off-camera flash held high. (*Robert Estall*)

connects to a flashgun. When the slave cell receives the light from the flash which is on the camera, it fires the flash to which it is connected. This happens so fast that all the flashguns go off virtually simultaneously. With the two flash-and-slave combinations each clipped to a high bookshelf in opposite corners of the room, a small on-camera flashgun will also fire the other two to provide a more even overall lighting effect. This avoids the usual result of a very washed-out looking foreground and under-exposed dark background.

Flash pictures outdoors

Using flash outdoors, especially in the daytime, seems particularly daft at first. However, it is as important to have even lighting for outdoor shots as it is to balance the contrast in light level for indoor pictures by available light. Using a

35 mm SLR camera; 24 mm lens; 64 ASA film; 1/15 sec; f/4;
direct flash. (*Robert Estall*)

flash is a particularly useful technique for
shooting portraits outdoors when the sun is at
its brightest. The technique is called *fill-in
flash*. It is the method by which the artificial
flash light is used in synchronization with the
sunlight to fill-in the shadow areas of the subject
with 'extra' light.

If fill-in flash was not used and you metered
and exposed for the most detail in the shadow
areas, the brightly lit areas would be completely washed out. If on the other hand you
exposed for the highlights, the darker areas
would be completely black. Since the light
cannot be taken away from the bright areas, it
must be added to the dark areas to provide the
balanced effect. Another advantage of this
technique in portrait shots is that your subject
will not have to face into the bright sun, and

therefore will not be squinting at the camera
with a prune-like expression.

If you can take the shot when the sun is to one
side of the subject's head, the sun will act as a
rim light and add a glow to the top of the subject's hair.

To determine what camera settings to use,
you must first set the correct shutter speed for
use with electronic flash. For most 35 mm
SLR cameras this will be 1/60 sec, but check your
camera's handbook to be certain. Then stand
the subject about 90 deg. to the sunlight with
one shoulder pointing in the direction of the
sun. You too should be standing about 90 deg.
to the sun and facing the subject. Then take a
normal exposure meter reading – remember
to keep the shutter speed dial set to the correct
x-sync speed. Note the lens aperture required
and set this on the lens.

Now the procedure varies slightly depending
on whether you are using a manual flashgun or
an automatic. If you are using a manual flashgun, set a film speed value on the gun's calculator which is about four times that of the film
you are using. Then opposite the f/stop figure
which you have set on your lens, note what the
flash-to-subject distance should be and position yourself accordingly. If you are too far
away, move in closer and place a layer of hand-
kerchief over the flashgun's reflector or even
attach the gun's wide-angle diffuser if it comes
so equipped.

If you are using an automatic flashgun,
simply set a film speed ASA value which is
about four times that of the film you are using,
on the gun's calculator. The gun will 'think'
that you are using a very fast film and so therefore
will not give out much light – just a little to fill
in the shadows on your subject, but not enough
to overpower the natural sunlight effect. The
secret of fill-in flash success is to do it in such a
way that no one can tell you have used flash –
unless they look at the person's eyes for the tell-
tale highlight spot.

Of course flash can be used outdoors at night.
In dull weather, you can get some interesting

35 mm SLR camera; 180 mm lens; 160 ASA film; 1/15 sec; f/2.8.

effects. Be a bit careful though, or the shot might look too unnatural – or over-exaggerate the effect and go for the bizarre. Use the flash-gun much as you would indoors if there is still a little daylight around. If it is pitch black at night then use the flashgun normally, except set a film speed ASA value which is about one quarter of the film speed you actually have in the camera. This is because a flashgun's power output is judged in an 'average room' situation and so depends on some reflective surfaces nearby – which obviously do not exist outdoors – hence the slight adjustment needed.

The same general philosophy of fill-in flash outdoors during the day can be used at night. For example, let us say you want a portrait of a friend standing by a fairly brightly lit fountain at night but not lit by the fountain's light.

The calculations are done in a different order however. First you can figure out what lens aperture is necessary for the flash exposure on your friend (remember you are outdoors, so use a film speed setting on your flash which is about one quarter that of the film you are actually using). Set this aperture on your lens. Then, leaving this aperture set on the lens, meter the light on the fountain and adjust only the shutter speed until correct exposure is indicated by the camera. Step back, re-compose the shot and fire. You will have to ask your friend to stand as steady as possible for the duration, but a little movement probably will not be noticed. The flash will more or less 'freeze' your friend's image on the film, while the shutter may continue to stay open for a second or two (whatever you set on the speed dial for the correct exposure) so that the fountain also receives the correct exposure. If your friend looks somewhat ghostly and transparent on the resulting picture, it will be because he or she moved slightly.

Night-time pictures

Night-time pictures add an exciting dimension to your photo album and extend your enjoy-

ment of photography. The minimum require-ment is a camera with film and a cable release, though some cameras with electronic shutters require an electronic remote release. Exposures have to be long – several seconds or even minutes – so unless you are good at finding nearby walls or benches or similar unmoving props, you will need a tripod. This will hold the camera absolutely still while the shutter is open and prevent subject blur. As tripods tend to be quite heavy and fairly cumbersome, you may consider a lighter, smaller, table-top tripod or a

monopod as a better alternative. But if you
get caught out one night without one of these,
you could try to keep your camera still by
holding it firmly against the wall of a building
or a lamp-post.

Composition may present something of a
problem with moving subjects, but most night-
time pictures depend on the colour and pattern
of lights to help make the picture outstanding.
Do not hesitate to go out in the rain either,
because the wet pavement will double the
apparent number of lights and form reflec-

35 mm SLR camera; 180 mm lens; 160 ASA film;
1/15 sec; f/2.8.

tions. Try to find a viewpoint which puts the
lights in such a position as to draw the eye into
the scene – much as you use the compositional
lines of a fence, etc., to draw the eye into a
landscape.

Unless you choose not to have any sky in the
picture, it is good to include some, but better
if it is not all pitch black. Try to shoot your night
pictures just after the sun sets or just before it
rises so that the sky still has some dramatic

35 mm SLR camera; 35 mm lens; 200 ASA film; 8 sec; f/5.6.
(*Allan Shriver*)

colour in it. At these times you can probably
trust your camera's exposure meter reading.

Exposure is sometimes a problem with night
pictures – the meter tries to give you an exposure
which will give you an evenly lit shot, rather
than the night-time appearance of mostly
dark areas with small areas of intense lighting.
The result is that your shots tend to look as if
they have been taken in dull daylight. To
avoid this, note what the light meter says and
give the shot about one stop less exposure by
closing down the aperture one f/number, say
from f/8 to f/11, or by using the next faster
shutter speed, say 1/60 sec instead of 1/30 sec.

In order to have a fair amount of detail in
sharp focus, the aperture will have to be quite
small, perhaps f/8 or so. This will usually mean
that quite a long shutter speed will be needed –
maybe 2 seconds with a 100 ASA film for a well-
lit street scene. Rather than worrying about

and waiting for every last pedestrian and car to stay away, just take the shot – any movement will add life to the picture. If you want a more creative effect, include a busy street in the picture and adjust your exposure so it requires a shutter speed of, say, 6 seconds; then the lights of the cars passing by will show up as coloured streamers in the photograph. If a pedestrian walks in front of your camera, it is unlikely that he will show up in the photo as long as he does not linger in front of the lens. This is because

he is not in the same spot long enough to receive sufficient light to register sharply on the film.

The light from a typical small amateur flash-gun is useless outdoors at night for distant details, but may help pick up nearby ones. Perhaps you want a person in the picture: establish what f/stop you need for a correct flash exposure and set this on the lens. Then take a light meter reading with this f/stop set on the lens or on the exposure meter if your camera cannot measure the light when that dim. Set

this speed on the camera's shutter speed dial – if it needs 4 seconds, then use the B setting and a cable release. Ask your subject to stay fairly still for 4 seconds and take the picture. The initial flash will give the correct exposure on the figure while the remaining long shutter speed time will give the background the correct exposure. However, try to avoid using flash where it might spoil the atmosphere of the shot, for example if you are trying to capture the look and mood of a bonfire; the artificial 'interference' of the flash kills the warm glow of the fire's light. Always try to think about the overall visual effect and mood of the photograph before implementing the various mechanical devices available to you.

OPPOSITE: 35 mm SLR camera; 50 mm lens; 64 ASA film; 4 sec; f/11. (*Allan Shriver*)

35 mm SLR camera; 50 mm lens; 160 ASA film; 1/125 sec; f/11.

Landscape pictures

Taking pictures of landscapes can be boringly easy or may cause time-consuming problems of composition. For example, to simply point the camera out over the clifftops and shoot is not doing justice to nature. Generally there is a particular part of a landscape which catches our attention and it is this detail which you should identify mentally as the main subject of the photograph, then build detail around it.

There are four mistakes which are frequently made: too much detail is included and most of it is too small to recognize; the picture is taken with the horizon bang in the middle so half the picture (sky) is a washed out area without points of interest; it is taken from a standing viewpoint; and, lastly, it is always taken framed

horizontally. Does this sound like your pictures? The problems are easily rectified. To make more exciting landscapes, simply hold the camera on its side for a vertical format shot and point it downward slightly more than usual.

It may be because we sleep lying down, i.e. horizontally, that the horizontal format appears more peaceful than the vertical to us. Consequently a horizontal format is better suited to a landscape which we want to appear peaceful, while a vertical format is better for a more psychologically moving image. There may be times when we want to capture the intensity of a stormy landscape and again, a vertical format would be good here. If there is a stormy sky with angry looking clouds, then tilt the camera up slightly, putting the horizon low and getting all the anger of the sky. You can even get such a dramatic sky on a bright sunny day on black and white film by shooting through a deep red filter.

Lens filters can help a landscape shot tremendously, provided you are not committed to shooting everything as nature would have it. A graduated filter can add a different colour to the land in your landscape while leaving the sky natural, or rotated around 180 deg., the sky can appear tinted with 'normal' detail in the bottom part of the shot.

If you wish to include the sun in the picture, first meter the exposure *without* including the sun or else the bright light will give you a silhouette effect – unless of course that is what you want. But *never* look at the sun directly through the camera's viewfinder or you may damage your eye. As an experiment, you could try intentionally under-exposing a shot on colour film during the day using a deep blue filter. This will give you what looks like a night-time shot and might save you having to wait for hours for the sun to set.

Try shooting landscapes at different times of the day and note the difference even the same scene has when lit with light of a different quality and angle. Remember that oblique or side-lighting best shows up depth and dimension. Late afternoon and early morning light tends to be a warmer yellow or orange than mid-day shadowless light. Also try to shoot at times other than just in good weather. Your raincoat is probably big enough for you and your camera; if not, then get a plastic bag for the camera. Go out while it is raining or immediately after and see what interesting landscapes you can take.

A landscape shot does not mean simply the whole of what your eyes see when pointed in the general direction of the horizon – take in some small details, too. Try focusing on some sparkling flowering shrubs or a glistening hedgerow right after a rainstorm. Immediately following a storm when the sun begins to shine through the clouds again, some great landscapes can be shot, especially if the sun is quite low.

While on the subject of rain and storms, many photographers have trouble with rainbows, the first problem being having a camera to hand, loaded with colour film. Rainbows are usually quite faint and offer little contrast between their bands and the dark grey background sky, so the camera will normally give an average exposure; sometimes this works, more often it does not. One way around the problem is to under-expose slide film by about $\frac{1}{2}$ to 1 f/stop; this will saturate the colours. The same will happen with colour negative film, but here it is better to over-expose by 1 to 2 f/stops.

The best way to get the brightest colours on slide film is to use a polarising filter. As well as its other properties mentioned in earlier pages of cutting through reflections, the filter also deepens the hues of colours slightly. It is the only filter which can be used with colour film to make a pale blue sky go deep blue without affecting other colours and so is great for countries with fairly pale summer skies. Unfortunately it will not make a grey sky go blue.

Close-up pictures

The area of close-up photography allows for a vast range of special effects and techniques,

Rangefinder 35 mm camera; 50 mm lens; 200 ASA film; 1/60 sec; f/8. (*Anne Price*)

many of which have been mentioned earlier. This makes it a particularly exciting field to work in although there are two main problems. One is getting enough light on the subject and the other is getting enough depth of field. The closer we get to a subject, the shorter the depth of field becomes, so for a longer depth of field we need a smaller aperture. With a small aperture there has to be either a lot of light or a long shutter speed. If we opt to shoot without flash, a shutter speed of, say, $\frac{1}{2}$ sec may be necessary with a 100 ASA film. This is too long to hand-hold the camera so a tripod or other steadying device is needed, although it may prove impractical, depending on your subject.

Getting very close to small objects also means that our body, camera, or both may be blocking the light from reaching the subject. In cases where this is not a problem, any close-up aid and lens will be suitable. However, if you do need to keep some distance from the subject, you will find that using extension tubes or a bellows focusing unit in conjunction with a short telephoto or medium-long tele lens will

give you the distance you need to allow brighter and more even lighting from all angles without the camera casting a shadow over the subject.

With very large subject magnifications, the depth of field is so small that the slightest movement of the lens towards or away from the subject will take the subject out of the sharp focus range (depth of field). This is when shooting from a tripod becomes necessary and focusing is accomplished with a *focusing rail* between camera and tripod.

If you do not need a very big magnification, say to fill the frame with a rose bloom, you can shoot with a hand-held camera. However, to get sufficient depth of field for the sharpest possible bloom, you may need the assistance of an electronic flashgun – even outdoors. You would then find that another accessory will come in handy which fits on to the front of your lens and has either one or two accessory shoes. Into these you can fit one or two small electronic flash units to give you sufficient light for the smallest possible aperture.

When focusing an SLR camera, you will see

OPPOSITE: 35 mm SLR camera; 200 mm lens; 64 ASA film; 1/500 sec; f/6. (*Allan Shriver*)

BELOW: 6 × 6 cm SLR camera; 80 mm lens; 160 ASA film; 1/250 sec; f/16; supplementary close-up lens. (*A. Knowles*)

in the viewfinder that the subject never looks completely in focus all over – this is because most SLRs offer the facility known as full-aperture viewing (and metering). So the lens iris diaphragm does not *stop down* until you fire the shutter. When focusing then, focus on the part of the subject which is closest to the lens. This is because the depth of field always extends slightly beyond the point of focus more than it extends in front of the point of focus.

Composition is usually less important in close-up pictures, and the limited depth of field prevents busy backgrounds from detracting from the importance of the main subject. However, if it is at all possible, try to include some object which is a known size as a point of comparison. The viewer may not realize just how close you had to get for that nice big picture of a subject unless he can relate its size to something he already knows.

Close-up photography also encompasses copying documents or other photographs for which you may have lost the original negative. A *close-up stand* may be helpful but you must ensure that the paper or print that you are

ABOVE: 35 mm SLR camera; 135 mm lens; 160 ASA film; 1/1000 sec; f/4; diffused daylight outdoors. (*Allan Shriver*)

BELOW: 35 mm SLR camera; 50 mm lens with +2 dioptre supplementary lens; 25 ASA film; 1/60 sec; f/16; electronic flash. (*Robert Estall*)

copying is held absolutely flat. Try using a piece of non-reflective glass or a heavy piece of plain glass; if you use the latter, carefully arrange your lights to avoid nasty reflections.

As with any other type of close-up photography, copying presents the problem of providing the greatest possible depth of field with the smallest possible aperture. So bright light is required; most copying stands on the market have two adjustable photoflood lamp-holding arms. With two 375 watt photofloods about 15 in (381 mm) from the subject and when using a 125 ASA film, a usual exposure is about 1/60 sec at f/16. When copying flat artwork or a document, be sure to align the camera square with the subject so it does not appear distorted and keystone shaped on the negative. Of course you do not need to have a copying stand, just pinning the paper to a wall will work, but it must be held flat and square to the camera. If you are shooting colour film also remember to use film which is balanced for your light source, (noted on the side of the film box), e.g. Type A film with 3400 K photoflood lamps, or use a colour correction filter.

Rangefinder cameras are a bit more difficult to use close to small subjects since the distance between their lens and viewfinder creates *parallax* error. However, usually a viewfinder's bright-line frame has parallax correction marks which help somewhat when adjusting the 'aim' of the camera on subjects at about 3 ft (0.9 m) from the camera. Three feet (0.9 m) is minimum focusing distance for this type of camera with no close-up aid on its lens.

ABOVE: 35 mm SLR camera; 180 mm lens; 64 ASA film; 1/250 sec; f/11.

Action pictures

Amateur photographers tend to make a particular error when taking action pictures; they use such a fast shutter speed that most moving subjects are stopped in their tracks and look completely lifeless. Try to avoid 'freezing' a fast subject unless absolutely necessary. It is pointless to show a picture of a 200 mph (322 kmph) car frozen on a racetrack if your intention was to convey speed. If you simply want to see details of the car, wait until it stops in the pits or paddock to shoot it.

The best way to convey action or movement is to allow either the main subject or the background to be blurred to some degree. Blur will depend either on subject movement, camera movement or both. If you cannot adjust the shutter on your camera for a slow speed, then perhaps you should try *panning*. Panning is keeping the camera trained on the subject, adjusting to its speed so that it remains constantly within the viewfinder. In this way the

35 mm SLR camera; 135 mm lens; 200 ASA film; 1/250 sec; f/8.

subject remains stationary relative to the film, so the subject is pictured still and clearly, but the background is moving relative to the film so it appears blurred. This approach yields a more convincing action picture than one in which the background is steady but the subject is blurred.

The secret to a good panning technique is three-fold: first, eliminate all the exposure variables by choosing your shutter speed and aperture settings, second, pan smoothly – choose the point where you want to take the picture (noting the background) before the subject gets there and squarely face this spot, then as the subject approaches, twist from the waist to face the subject, keeping it in the viewfinder until it reaches your chosen spot and gently fire the shutter while continuing to follow the subject momentarily – follow

through; lastly, pre-focus to avoid last second focus adjustments which might make you miss the shot. This is easy to do when you pick your chosen spot; focus the lens on this spot and do not be tempted to change the focus setting – leave it there. As the subject approaches, it will become larger in the viewfinder and sharper. When it reaches your spot, take the picture, but remember to follow through. Also remember not to jab at the shutter release button. It is tempting to do this, particularly if the subject is moving quite fast, but is likely to cause camera shake and a blurred subject. Instead, simply press the shutter release button gently and firmly.

Another way to convey movement in frozen-action pictures, if you cannot set a fast speed on your camera, is to shoot the subject at the peak of action or at the point where it looks off-balance. One obvious example is of a child on a swing; if you shoot at the bottom of the swing's travel, the child might be blurred, because the swing is moving quickly. So you can try shooting when the child is at the top of the swing's travel when it is relatively stationary. However, this may entail finding a more unusual viewpoint if you want to see the child's face clearly. Shooting at the peak of the action means that a very slow shutter speed can be used; this could be especially handy when shooting a moving subject in dim light when the exposure demands both a wide aperture and a slow shutter speed.

Composition can also add to the impression of movement or simply of instability. If your subject looks too staid and you want to pep it up a bit, try tilting one end of the camera down slightly. It is surprising how much difference this will make. Portraits are often greatly enhanced by this little trick, but it can help action pictures too, even if the subject is moving quite fast anyway.

Freezing the fastest subjects is limited to using the fastest possible shutter speed; sometimes your camera's top speed, be it 1/500 sec, 1/1000 sec or even 1/2000 sec, is still not fast enough. Then, depending on the subject, you may like to try using flash to stop the subject instead. The duration of the light flash from most electronic flashguns is about 1/1000 sec at its slowest. Depending on the aperture used with an automatic exposure gun and the distance of the subject, it can be as fast as about 1/50 000 sec – this is fast enough to stop a drop of water falling, a party balloon bursting, or even a bullet. Without the aid of sophisticated timing and triggering equipment, your chances of success depend on your coordination between, for example, hitting a balloon with a pin and triggering the camera's shutter, virtually at the same instant. A bit of practice with an empty camera and a box of balloons will give you a sense of the timing you will need. Set the correct aperture and shutter speed for the flash exposure and try a few pictures in a dimly lit room. The reason the room should be fairly dim is to prevent distracting background detail from registering on the film.

35 mm SLR camera; 180 mm lens; 200 ASA film; 1/125; f/8

35 mm SLR camera; 50 mm lens; 200 ASA film; 1/125 sec; f/8.

Family album pictures

Most pictures can go into the family album but the accent should be on the members of the family as individuals and groups, rather than holiday landscape scenes. When a child reaches adulthood, a personalized album of pictures relating to his or her own life is a welcome gift.

Although people should generally feature in all pictures, especially in potentially boring landscapes, only members of your own family and very close friends should really feature in the family album. And all members of the family, not just dad, should be enthusiastically encouraged to contribute photos to the album to make it truly an album for and about the family.

The family album should have four strong elements – completeness, variety, continuity and sensitivity. It should show 'the complete family story'; pictures should do more than just illustrate the various members of the family, they should capture each of those highly individual human beings in a vast array of places, moods and attitudes. Children present a never ending photographic saga and mum is probably best placed to get shots of the kids as they grow up while they are still at home. Make sure that there is always a loaded camera set and ready for that unexpected 'grab shot'. The completeness depends on showing all the members of the family when they are happy as well as when the tears flow, or the plates fly. Completeness also depends on getting shots of all those important 'firsts' in the lives of children, such as the first haircut, the first birthday party, the first tricycle.

Having a wide variety of pictures in the album keeps it lively and also is more likely to hold the attention of the initially less interested, especially fidgeting youngsters and teenagers. And it is these younger members of the family, with their seemingly innate talent for catching people at their worst or at their funniest, who have a particularly important role to play in contributing pictures to the family album. No age is too young to start; with the inexpensive and uncomplicated

cameras around, if a child can hold the camera up, he can start taking pictures. A nice idea is to initiate photography contests within the family and award prizes for the best monthly or annual contribution to the album.

Continuity is also an important factor. Small kids grow up so very fast that a good picture every week or two is not too much. As the child develops his or her own personality, the scope for pictures explodes. Pictures of the kids (and mum and dad, too) with spaghetti on their face, playing outdoors, engrossed in thought, studying homework, eating, sleeping, enjoying a holiday are just a few of the possibilities. As the children grow older, maybe only a handful of pictures each year need get into the album, but one per year of each person should be the absolute minimum. The album should also include an annual portrait of the whole family taken by one member of the family (using the delayed shutter self-timer) or by a professional. These serve to round-out the pictures of the family fragments

ABOVE: 35 mm SLR camera; 50 mm lens; 160 ASA film; 1/15 sec; f/2.

BELOW: 35 mm SLR camera; 50 mm lens; 160 ASA film; 1/60 sec; f/5.6.

and form a thread running through the album. Remember that the album should not be just pictures of the kids; the kids should be encouraged to take shots of both of you, too, and of each other. This embodies the last element of the family album – sensitivity. It is easy to catch someone out when they are not expecting a camera to be pointing in their direction – *candid* shots are often better than the more formal, posed ones – but if someone only photographs you when you are looking dreadful, perhaps you should find out why. Pictures of anyone can look good if both photographer and subject cooperate, just as in any professional photographer/model relationship.

Shooting a lot of pictures does not necessarily mean that you all need your own cameras, but a simple and quick-to-use one might be more handy for a mother with small kids or for the kids themselves. Too many fathers keep their treasured and expensive toys well away from the hands of their children, but how better to inspire good photography and creativity than with a more versatile camera and a few tips from someone with more experience. In addition, the more you shoot around the house, the less camera-shy the family becomes and the less prone to showing off. They will relax to the point that some really true-to-character shots become possible. It is somehow reassuring to look at a good picture of someone you know and to think that it captures him perfectly.

The family album does not have to be limited to photographs – other items can creep in too, for example, a lock of the new baby's hair, a particularly good (or bad) school report card. Pictures sometimes speak for themselves, but it may aid fading memories to jot a few notes under one or two, say the holiday shots. You may choose to be brief and factual, noting simply date and location, or you may prefer longer comments discussing why there is a funny expression on someone's face or how the baby especially preferred men with beards, and so on. If a picture is not particularly good, you may want to note why you included it, for example, it may have been taken on the day the baby said his first word.

Portrait pictures

Ideally, portraits should communicate to the viewer not simply what the subject looks like, but also something about the person, what he or she is like as a human being. A portrait need not be formal and posed, nor should it always be just a facial picture. It can successfully include some item of particular relevance to that person – for a child this might be his favourite toy, for a smoker it may be his pipe, for a photographer, his camera or for a teenager, his record collection. Also a portrait may be of more than one person. It may include the whole family or simply a mother and her baby. By definition a portrait should be a vivid graphic description of the 'sitter' which is best caught (and it may be a fleeting expression which must, indeed, be caught) when the photographer is totally familiar with his camera (so as not to waste time and important shots) and also familiar with the sitter.

In cases where you are taking a portrait of someone who is camera-shy and who you are relatively unfamiliar with, it is useful to follow the person around for a while, shooting without film in the camera. In this way the idea of your taking a photograph of them will soon lose its novelty and you will be able to tell when they are relaxed and presenting a natural image of themselves. Encourage a continuous dialogue, but beware of getting half-open mouths. Helping your sitter to be unselfconscious will eliminate posed and contrived expressions and attitudes.

A sculptor's work says something about both the sculptor and his relationship to his model; in the same way, your photographs say something about you. In a portrait photo, the person need not always be the largest element, although this is often the case. Posture and general bodily attitudes say a lot about a person and as such, should be studied and highlighted by your photo. Take a few pictures of the person's face if you wish, but also make portraits to the waist and full-length shots too. And try taking a few from low down or from a high viewpoint. Use what you know about the more

35 mm SLR camera; 50 mm lens; 200 ASA film;
1/60 sec; f/4.

dynamic, vertical-format shots to inject some of the person's character into the portrait, or use a horizontal frame if you want the image of the person to appear calm and sedate.

Consider the expression 'looking up to someone'. It implies that one person is impressed by another, that he or she is important to them and respected by them. The camera can reflect all these attitudes, too – it can look up towards a person, if that is how you wish to portray him. And rather than looking down on children with your camera, since children have such a unique viewpoint on the world, try kneeling down and taking pictures of them from their own level.

Lighting, too, plays an important role, since strong light from one direction, say a spotlight, can be considered 'cruel', showing up a person's every wrinkle, spot and blemish. A softer, *diffused light* makes for a more flattering portrait, just as does attaching a soft-focus filter to the lens. These devices are traditionally used for portraits of women and children. What are known as *high-key* portraits also tend to be more flattering. A high-key photo is one in which most tones run from mid-grey to white, whereas a *low-key* photo has most tones running from mid-grey to black.

Many formal portraits rely on complex lighting set-ups. These may well be too expensive and a hindrance to the amateur. The easiest light to use is soft but quite bright daylight streaming through a window, perhaps diffused by a thin curtain. With the person sitting near the window to 45–90 deg., you will get a good range of highlight and shadow tones; a card reflector may also be used to fill in or somewhat lighten the shadows, too, for a more evenly lit picture. And of course the usual daylight colour film can still be used.

People often want two good portraits of themselves – one being the image they would like to project (as they would like others to see them), and the other a less formal portrait, more as they really are in private. The former shot will no doubt appear somewhat stiff and contrived, but will nevertheless please the sitter more than the more candid shot. It is likely, however, that you as photographer will prefer the other.

Camera aids and accessories are less important here, but be wary of getting too close to a face with a standard focal length lens (or a wide-angle), because the closer you get, the more distorted the perspective becomes. If you want a good full-face portrait, it is best to use a telephoto lens and stand slightly farther back from the subject. This presents a much more natural perspective yet keeps the subject large in the frame.

35 mm SLR camera; 50 mm lens; 160 ASA film; 1/15 sec; f/1.

Children pictures

Good pictures of children come in two categories, the ridiculously easy and the frustratingly difficult. Either you need a child's total cooperation or you simply 'shoot around them' getting what you can. It is a bit unfair to ask a small child to pose on request, as what you had in mind will probably not suit their way of thinking.

For babies and very young children, avoid bright light – this includes electronic flash, flashcubes and even direct sunlight if you can. Instead, use the fastest speed film you can in less bright but soft, even light. If need be, special processing can artificially provide a faster than normal film; e.g. set your camera's film speed dial to 1600 ASA when using a 400 ASA film in your camera, but be sure to tell the processor that you have 'up-rated' the film to 1600 ASA (or the pictures will come out far too dark). What will happen, however, is that the pictures will appear quite grainy.

Young children are often perfectly content to play with a favourite toy while you play with your camera. Above all, you must be prepared to shoot at any time, but you may easily become frustrated at waiting and waiting until 'the right shot' happens. Instead, try setting the camera on a tripod or similar base (out of the child's reach) and use a long cable release or *air bulb release* connected to the shutter button. This will allow you to talk to a friend or read a book until the picture you are looking for 'happens'; then just squeeze the bulb or press the cable release and the picture should be yours.

Babies are probably at their most natural and appealing when being held by their mothers, and here, too, a soft-focus filter on the front of the lens will render a gentler, more moving photograph, especially with soft diffused day lighting from a window.

Slightly older children develop incredibly fast and seem to change from week to week. You should try to photograph them almost every week to put together a good visual record of their growing up. Later, when they change

35 mm SLR camera; 50 mm lens; 200 ASA film; 1/15 sec; f/2.

less rapidly, pictures from month to month or a selection each year should suffice. Catch children when they are unaware of you – candid shots are really the best of kids. All times are appropriate – when they are playing, crying, sleeping, laughing, eating; when they are having a bath, enjoying their first party, hating getting their hair cut, cuddling a friend, and all the other myriad of moments.

It is valuable to complete the story of children's developing lives by doing more than just photographing them. Include in the pictures items (or friends, or places) that are important to them. For a new-born baby it is his bottle, perhaps for an older child his teddy bear, and for a teenager his model airplane collection. An additional bonus is that children will probably be more willing to participate in front of the camera if they can have some of the things that they care about to hand. Also, they

OPPOSITE: 35 mm SLR camera; 70–260 mm zoom lens set at 90 mm; 64 ASA film; 1/60 sec; f/16. (*Allan Shriver*)

ABOVE: 35 mm SLR camera; 180 mm lens; 64 ASA film; 1/250 sec; f/11.

will be more natural when in their own environment. You may find, for example, that children are more cooperative when they play host to you as guest in their territory (their room or playhouse) and so feel that they, not you, are in charge of the whole show.

To help to put even the most timid child at ease, try getting him to talk about himself or his favourite topic – toys, school, girls, and so on. Another method which sometimes works is to pretend that you are using a TV camera and they are giving you a guided tour of their territory; this relaxes them, keeps them moving (so you have a choice of types of shots and expressions and backgrounds) and keeps them more interested. Of course different methods work better on different children, but the main task is to be ready, not to expect too much from them, not to depend on elaborate lighting set-ups, and to be familiar with your camera. When the shot you want presents itself you should be ready to take it instantly rather than calling a halt while you fiddle with your speed and aperture settings. This is when an automatic exposure camera can be a boon, but if you preset these on a manual camera you should be all right. Keep the lighting simple, keep the equipment simple, and keep the background simple. If you are shooting outdoors this simply means getting up high to shoot downwards and using the grass as a background or getting down low and using the sky as a background. If you are indoors, you may have to take down a picture from the wall or move a chair. Above all, avoid the straightforward, characterless mug shot with the child standing absolutely still, up against a wall directly facing the camera.

Animal pictures

In some ways animals are even more difficult subjects than children, since children can at least hear your pleas for cooperation whether or not they heed them, while animals do have to be 'caught' in the act and cannot be posed.

For most of us, animal pictures are limited to shots of our pets and of zoo animals. The more modern open zoos or safari parks provide a much more natural environment in which to picture the animals. If you cannot roll down your car window to shoot, then try fitting a polarizing filter on the lens to cut the reflections from inside the car or hold a dark coat behind you or over your head (and camera) right up against the window. Some safari parks have special vans which take you around and from which you can safely and comfortably shoot pictures of the animals.

A telephoto lens will help to magnify images of small and distant animals so they are not just specks in the middle of your picture when you get them back from the processor. If you do not have a tele lens but your camera does have an interchangeable lens, then you could try using a teleconverter as mentioned in the section on accessories. A long lens will call for a fairly fast shutter speed to prevent subject blur through camera-shake and to get sharp pictures of the animals if they are running – unless you pan with them. It is advisable to use a fairly *fast film*, say from 125 ASA to 400 ASA; use one from the upper end of the scale if it is a dull day.

You will probably have to rely on the available light whether you are outdoors or in, since flash will either not reach far enough or, if it does, may frighten the subject even farther out of range. Remember that if you are shooting colour film indoors at a zoo the lighting may produce a slightly green or orange colour cast on your pictures unless you use daylight colour film with a correction filter on the front of your lens. These filters may have a filter factor calling

35 mm SLR camera; 50 mm lens; 200 ASA film; 1/60 sec; f/4.

ABOVE: 35 mm SLR camera; 135 mm lens; 64 ASA film; 1/1000 sec; f/4. (*Allan Shriver*)

ABOVE RIGHT: 35 mm SLR camera; 135 mm lens; 64 ASA film; 1/125 sec; f/11. (*Allan Shriver*)

for up to $1\frac{1}{2}$/stops more exposure since they absorb some light, which makes an even better case for using a 400 ASA film.

If you are shooting animals in the zoo, it may be difficult to reach a vantage point where you can shoot straight into the cage without having to shoot through a wire fence. If you must shoot through a fence, it is better to use a wide aperture (to limit the depth of field) which will blur both the background and the

immediate foreground, i.e. the fence. The background will become less distracting and the fence may seem to disappear altogether. You should get the camera's lens as close to the fence as possible; you may even find that the lens will almost 'see' between the weave of the wire which would be better still. If you can get right up to the fence but your lens will not fit between the fence's weave, use an aperture which has the approximate physical size of the holes formed by the wires. This way the image-forming rays of light (taken from the central portion of the lens) come between the wires, and you won't have an ugly fence in your picture. If you remain some distance from the fence, it will almost disappear from the photo when you use the widest aperture. However, since it is still there (only out of focus) it will give your pictures a lower contrast so they may look a bit duller than the bright day you remembered.

OPPOSITE: With colour slide film and high contrast lighting such as this, an incident light reading is preferred by many photographers.

ABOVE: 35 mm SLR camera; 50 mm lens; 64 ASA film; 1/125 sec; f/8. (*Robert Estall*)

All animals seem to have their own, sometimes quite distinct, personalities. These become apparent the more you become familiar with them, be they your pets or zoo animals. Three of the most rewarding times for pictures of zoo animals, especially, is when they are just waking up in the morning (if you can get there in time), when they are being fed and when they are playing with or attending to their young.

As with taking pictures of children, try to get a variety of shots – when the animals are eating, sleeping, playing, or in odd places (a pet cat in a small cardboard box) or when they have unusual expressions (a group of monkeys 'conferring' in their cage). With pets, the finished photo will benefit if they are taken with their favourite playthings, in familiar surroundings or in a natural pose, like resting in their basket, for example. Above all, try to get shots which look natural. Do not try to get your pet to perform miracle tricks in front of your lens. And, as with very small children, try a few shots from their viewpoint, low to the ground – this will not only look more natural but will provide a better perspective and possibly a less cluttered background.

Glossary

Agitation The gentle swirling action used when developing a film to ensure that the active ingredients stay well distributed throughout the film developing tank during processing.

Air bulb release An accessory used in place of a conventional cable release to trigger the camera shutter without having to touch the camera. It is a long tube with a bulb on the end which you squeeze to take the picture.

Aperture The opening in a lens made by several overlapping metal blades to control the amount of light passing through the lens to the film.

Aperture-priority The exposure mode of an automatic exposure camera; once the lens aperture has been set by the photographer, the camera will give a correct exposure by choosing the shutter speed itself.

Aperture-priority auto-only SLR A type of single lens reflex camera which operates in the aperture-priority mode, but does not have manual shutter speed override – the photographer cannot choose whatever speed he wants.

ASA The abbreviation for the American Standards Association whose numerical system has been adopted for the rating of film emulsions so that the photographer knows how sensitive the film is to light.

Available light The light which already exists naturally outdoors or indoors without adding to it by artificial means, e.g. an electronic flashgun.

B setting For long time exposures, the B setting is selected on the camera's shutter speed dial – the shutter then stays open as long as the cable release button is held down which holds the shutter button down.

Back-light The lighting for a picture as the camera faces the light source with the subject between the camera and light source.

Back-light compensation control As back-light can cause under-exposed subjects, this control can be set on some cameras to give the shot extra exposure; for extra exposure it is set to the ' + ' side of the normal, 0 or 1X index; some controls also have '–' factors which can be set.

Bounce flash To aim electronic flash at the ceiling or wall so that the surface reflects the light on to the subject; provides a slightly softer light.

Candids Shots taken of subjects unaware of being photographed

Cartridge A plastic easy-load holder for 110 and 126 film; cartridge film does not need to be rewound before unloading it from the camera.

Cassette A metal canister film holder for 35mm film; this film must be rewound back into the cassette after all the shots have been taken; if the camera back is opened before the film is rewound, the film will be ruined.

CC filter Colour correction or colour compensation filter – used on the lens to correct the colour temperature of the light passing through to the film to the correct range for which the film is made; provides 'natural' colours on subjects under 'unnatural' lighting, i.e. when shooting indoor subjects under tungsten lighting with Daylight film in the camera.

Close-up stand This is an accessory, sometimes also called a macro stand, which may be used with a bellows unit or other close-up aid to hold a small subject (perhaps a stamp, etc.) in a fixed position and at a fixed distance from the camera lens.

Colour negative film Film used for colour prints; must be printed on to paper.

Colour slides Small transparent images which are the actual pieces of film from the camera which have been mounted in cardboard or plastic mounts after processing.

Colour temperature The measure of the colour quality of light; measured in degrees on the Kelvin scale; the higher the number, the more blue the light, the lower the number the more orange the light.

Colour transparency film The film used for colour slides.

Compact The term most often refers to the 35mm non-reflex type of camera, though in recent years due to the diminishing size of 35mm SLR cameras, some SLRs are called Compact SLRs.

Composition The arrangement of the visual elements of a picture and the relationship between the main subject, foreground and background.

Contrast The amount of difference between black and white in terms of the range of grey tones between black and white; high contrast means fewer grey tones.

Contrast filter A lens attachment used to control the amount of contrast recorded by black and white film.

Daylight film Film which is designed to give correct colours when exposed to daylight illumination; when exposed to tungsten lighting (as indoors in a home) the pictures will appear yellow.

Dedicated flashgun A flash unit which is designed to work with a particular camera so that it can automatically set the correct x-sync speed when the flash is ready to fire; some have other advantages as well, such as correct flash function confirmation in the camera viewfinder.

Depth of field The amount of distance between the nearest part and the farthest part of the scene which will be acceptably sharp; it extends both in front of and behind the subject focused on, but twice as much area behind the subject is in focus than in front of it.

Depth of field preview A means on some cameras by which the depth of field of the subject can be seen on the viewfinder's focusing screen.

Developer A chemical which reacts with film to form an image.

Diffused lighting Lighting which is soft and even, coming from all directions towards the subject; diffused lighting shows up few shadows on the subject.

DIN Deutsch Industrie Norm, the German industrial standards organisation which operates much like the ASA and which has also devised a numerical film speed rating system.

Electronic flashgun A small, lightweight, portable light source which usually runs off a few small batteries to help take pictures where available light is too dim.

Emulsion The light sensitive coating on film and photographic printing paper.

Fast film Film which is very sensitive to light (with a relatively high film speed number) and which is especially suited for shooting in dim light.

Fill-in flash Technique of using electronic flash when outdoors to lighten the shadow areas of the subject.

Film speed The numerical rating system by which we know how sensitive to light a particular film is; measured by the ASA (also sometimes BSI or ISO) or DIN system, the higher the number, the more sensitive to light, and the more suitable it is for use in dim light.

Filter A camera lens attachment for controlling the quality, quantity or special effects of the light passing through the lens.

Filter factor The amount by which the filter reduces the quantity of light passing through it; a factor of $\times 2$ requires twice the normal (non-filter) exposure to be given, hence the lens aperture must be opened up (increased) by one f/stop, say from f/8 to f/5.6.

Fixer The chemical which makes permanent an image on film rendered visible by the developer.

Flare Non-image-forming light which bounces around inside a lens and which subsequently lowers the contrast of the picture generally; it may produce geometric shapes on the picture which are formed by the non-image-forming light passing through the lens iris diaphragm leaving an image of the diaphragm blade formation on the film.

f/number The number given to a particular aperture size; the greater the number, the narrower or smaller the aperture size; also called an f/stop.

Focal length A measurement used to denote the image magnification or reduction power of a lens;

each film format has its own 'standard' focal length lens which gives a picture having a view most like that of the human eyes.

Focusing rail This is usually a flat track which is used between a tripod and a bellows unit. When using a bellows for extreme magnifications of small subjects, the image is focused not with the lens' focusing ring, but by adjusting the lens-to-subject distance – without disturbing the bellows extension (which would upset any pre-set magnification factor, *if* a specific factor is required).

Format This describes either the dimensions of the film's image frame size or whether the rectangular frame is orientated horizontally or vertically.

f/stop Another term for f/number.

Grain The visible lumps of developed silver particles of an emulsion which make up a picture's image; many grains together make a black area, a few make a grey area, none leave that part of the picture white; a grainy picture has a rough, speckled, gravelly appearance.

Guide Number The number used to denote the strength of a light source; given in relation to feet or metres and a film speed; e.g. 30 (metres at 100 ASA) which is equivalent to 98 (feet at 100 ASA). The correct lens aperture to use with the light source is determined by dividing the Guide Number by the flash-to-subject distance and using the nearest numerical f/number on the lens aperture ring.

Hard lighting Lighting from a limited direction which makes irregular surfaces cast deep shadows.

High contrast An image in which there are few shades of grey between black and white.

High key A type of lighting in which the majority of the tones in the image are in the mid-grey to white tonal range.

Hot shoe The clip into which a camera accessory is fitted; most often used for mounting electronic flash which then does not also have to be connected to a separate socket by a lead; the hot shoe provides both electrical and physical connections.

Image contrast See Contrast.

Incident light Light which falls on the subject; measuring the incident light on a subject is often more accurate than the more usual reflected light measurement method.

Infinity Photographically it is the focusing distance beyond which a lens cannot be focused; i.e. if the infinity focus setting of a lens is at the 50 feet (15 m) point, then all subjects beyond 50 feet (15 m) will also be in focus when the infinity mark (∞) is set at the focusing index line.

Iris diaphragm The adjustable structure of several overlapping metal leaves or blades in a lens to form an aperture through which light passes to the film.

Kelvin Abbreviated as K, the temperature scale used to measure colour temperature – the colour quality of light.

Lens aperture See Aperture.

Lens hood A lens attachment which shades the lens' front element from oblique light rays which could cause flare.

Light box An illuminated box used to help sort slides.

Low contrast An image in which there are few shades of grey between black and white.

Low key Type of lighting in which the majority of the tones in the image are in the mid-grey to black tonal range.

Manual exposure override The facility on some automatic exposure cameras whereby the photographer can set whatever combination of both lens aperture and shutter speed he requires for the desired effect.

Monochrome This means 'one colour', but refers mainly to black and white images, black and white prints and black and white film.

Montage An image formed by pasting together bits of several unrelated images.

Multi-mode SLR This refers to a single lens reflex camera which offers the user several exposure mode choices such as aperture-priority automatic exposure, shutter-priority auto exposure and manual exposure.

Negative An image in which the 'true' tones are reversed, white subjects appear black and black subjects appear white; also refers to the piece of film used to make a print.

Non-reflex camera A camera in which the viewfinder does not use a mirror and condensor system to provide the photographer with an image of the subject as the camera lens sees it; many non-reflex cameras may also be called rangefinder cameras whether or not they have a rangefinder.

Normal lens See Standard lens.

Over-exposure Exposing the film to too much light; the picture will then appear washed-out.

Panning Capturing a moving subject with a slow shutter speed for a 'frozen' subject and a blurred background by following the subject in the camera's viewfinder while making the exposure.

Parallax The difference in viewpoint between that of the camera lens and the camera viewfinder when it is focused on very close subjects; without correction for this difference (called parallax error) part of the subject will be cut off.

Pocket camera This often refers to 110 format cameras, or a pocketable camera of any format.

Positive film Film for positive (not negative) images; also called transparency film or slide film; see Colour slides.

Printing The process of exposing photographic paper to light which is shone through a film negative; also called enlarging since the image on paper is enlarged from the negative size.

Programmed exposure mode The exposure mode used by some cameras in which both the lens aperture and shutter speed are automatically set as the light varies to give the correct exposure on film.

Pushing film See Up-rating film.

Rangefinder The mechanism in some cameras which aids focusing by comparing two images of the same subject seen from slightly different viewpoints (as in human binocular vision) in order to find the distance of the subject so that the lens is focused correctly to render that subject sharp.

Rangefinder camera A camera which has a rangefinder focusing aid; also sometimes called a non-reflex camera or a compact camera, though the latter does not always have a rangefinder focusing aid.

Red-eye The appearance of people in colour prints having red eyes due to the flash source being very close to the camera's lens when the picture was taken.

Reflected light Light which is reflected by the subject towards the camera; most cameras with built-in exposure meters and hand-held exposure meters read reflected light for exposure measurement.

Reflex camera A camera which uses a mirror and condensor system to provide the photographer with an image of the subject as the camera's lens sees it.

Reversal film Another name for slide film; see Colour slides.

Reversal print A print made directly from enlarging a slide without first having to make a negative.

Rule of thirds A rule of composition that says if an image were to be divided by lines into equal thirds vertically and horizontally, the main subject of the photo should lie at one of the four points where two of the lines bisect.

Shutter The moving blades mechanism of a camera which controls the exposure time.

Shutter-priority The exposure mode of an automatic exposure camera which needs to have its shutter speed set first by the photographer, then the camera gives a correct exposure by choosing the aperture itself.

Shutter speed The fraction of a second that the shutter remains open allowing light through to reach the film to make the picture; on most cameras the speed is marked only by the fraction's denominator, i.e. a speed of 1/60 sec. is marked as 60.

Silica gel A packet of crystals which helps keep the air surrounding it free of moisture; good to pack in your camera bag and with camera and film when being stored for any lengthy time.

Skylight filter A lens filter fitted to protect a lens front element from dust and fingerprints and to help reduce the blueing effect of haze in the distance of landscape shots and in shady areas on sunny days.

Slave unit A small accessory used with a secondary flashgun which fires that gun when it receives light from the main (on-camera) flashgun.

Slide film See Colour slides.

Slow film Film which is relatively not very sensitive to light (with a relatively low film speed (ASA) number) and which is more suited to shooting in bright light; can be blown up with less noticeable grain for an apparently sharper picture than fast film would give under the same circumstances.

SLR Single lens reflex, a type of camera which uses a pentaprism to provide a right-side-up and right-way-round image of the subject exactly as the lens sees it; lenses can be changed on practically all SLR cameras.

Soft focus The technique of shooting a 'romantic' mood picture by using soft diffused lighting and probably a lens filter which slightly blurs fine detail.

Soft light Lighting which is diffused and casts no pronounced shadows; see Diffused lighting.

Standard lens The lens of a particular focal length (approximately that of the diagonal of the film frame it covers) which gives a view which is most like that of human vision; each film frame format has its own standard lens focal length – for the 35 mm film format which has a frame size of 24×36 mm, the standard lens' focal length is about 50 mm.

Stop bath The chemical solution sometimes used when processing film or paper (prints) to neutralise the effect of the developer before moving on to the fixer processing stage; it prevents the fixer from being contaminated by developer left on the film or paper.

Stop down A term used to describe the action of closing the lens aperture from the widest (full aperture) setting to that which you intend to use for your picture. Some camera metering systems require that the exposure reading is taken not at the lens' maximum (widest) aperture (which is the usual case), but when the lens aperture is closed to the value you want to use for that picture.

Teleconverter An accessory used between the camera and its lens to effectively increase the focal length of the lens it is used with; a $\times 2$ teleconverter used with a 50 mm lens would give pictures having the same effect as if they had been taken with a 100 mm lens (50 mm $\times$ 2 = 100 mm).

Telephoto lens A lens having a focal length longer than that of the standard lens for that format.

Thyristor A type of electronic switch used to conserve battery power in electronic flashguns by limiting the energy output of the capacitor to only that which is needed to make the correct amount of light for the correct exposure.

Time exposure The term loosely used for any exposure which is longer than, say, about 1 second or so.

TLR Twin lens reflex, a type of camera (sometimes also called a roll film camera – though not the only type of roll film camera) which has a lower picture-taking lens and a second upper image-viewing lens; it is a true reflex camera though few cameras of this type had interchangeable lenses, and the viewfinder's image, though right-side-up, is laterally reversed left to right.

Transparencies Another term for slides.

TTL The abbreviation for through-the-lens; often refers to a camera's ability to provide exposure metering measured TTL and/or to provide a viewfinder focusing image TTL.

Tungsten film Film which has been designed to render 'true' colours when exposed to light from a tungsten light source; Type B Tungsten film is balanced for light from sources having a colour temperature of about 3200 K, while Type A film is balanced for correct colour rendition when exposed to photoflood lamps of about 3400 K.

Under-exposure Exposing the film to too little light; the picture will then appear dark.

Up-rating film Artificially making the film more sensitive to dim light levels by doubling and possibly re-doubling the ASA number; in fact, it is being under-exposed and then over-developed later to compensate; this creates very grainy and high contrast images.

UV Ultra-violet light of a very high wavelength which tends to give the distant parts of landscape pictures a blue tone; also gives colours shot in the shade a partial blue tone (rectified by using a UV, haze or Skylight lens filter).

Wide-angle lens A lens having a focal length longer than that of the standard lens for that format; a lens having a wide angle of view.

X-sync socket The socket on some cameras into which the flashgun's lead must be connected so that the shutter and flash are correctly synchronized to go off together.

X-sync speed The shutter speed necessary on SLR cameras so that the shutter is completely open when the flash goes off; most horizontally-travelling focal plane shutters have an x-sync of 1/60 sec, while most vertically-travelling focal plane shutters have a speed between 1/90 sec to 1/125 sec, depending on the exact shutter design.

Zoom lens A lens having an adjustable focal length; most zoom lenses have a range which is telephoto; a 70–210 mm focal length range is typical for a telephoto zoom; other 200 m ranges may be 28–50 mm, 35–85 mm, etc.